The Barony of Castleknock

A HISTORY

The Barony of Castleknock

A HISTORY

JIM LACEY

The
History
Press
Ireland

First published 2015

The History Press Ireland
50 City Quay
Dublin 2
Ireland
www.thehistorypress.ie

British Library Cataloguing in Publication Data.
A catalogue record for this book is available from the British Library.

ISBN 978 1 84588 878 7

Typesetting and origination by The History Press
Printed in Malta by Melita Press

CONTENTS

INTRODUCTION

The aim of this work was to assemble a collection of the drawings, prints, paintings, maps and photographs relating to Blanchardstown, Castleknock and their hinterland to effectively illustrate the story of this historical part of County Dublin.

The area covered in the book embraces the land between the Great North Road in the east to the River Liffey in the west and from Cabra Cross in the south to the Meath border. The area is almost synonymous with the Barony of Castleknock. The Barony of Castleknock contains eight civil parishes. I have included six of these, centring on Blanchardstown and Castleknock. The civil parish of Ward and the civil parish of St James in Dublin city were in my opinion (and I may be wrong) somewhat remote in both distance and interaction from the Blanchardstown-Castleknock hub to include in this study. Similarly, part of the civil parish of Finglas around St Margaret's village and Finglas village would have more relevance to a book based on the parishes of Finglas and Glasnevin. These areas have a history going back to St Canice and St Mobhí and are worthy of a work of pictorial history in their own right.

Castleknock and Blanchardstown are very typical clustered villages of the type encountered in Britain and most of Western Europe that are usually centred on a church. However, three areas we also encounter in this book are linear villages: Strawberry Beds, which follows the line of the River Liffey; Blackhorse Lane or Avenue, which follows the line of a transport route, the old Coach Road to Navan; and finally Clonsilla, which follows the line of the Royal Canal, albeit with its back to the canal. Linear villages are more common in Ireland than in England due to the different agricultural practices in Celtic Ireland and the way villages developed here.

In the case of Blackhorse Lane, it stretches all the way from the urban North Circular Road to semi-rural Ashtown. The Strawberry Beds stretches from Knockmaroon along the line of the River Liffey almost to Lucan. Clonsilla is not as long as the previous two examples and there is a little clustering midway.

Castleknock, Blanchardstown and the surrounding areas feature prominently in the history of Ireland. The area of Castleknock around St Vincent's College and the old castle has a history dating back to antiquity. According to the *Lebor Gabála Érenn*, the early Milesian settlers were associated with the area and legend has it that Cumhall, father of Fionn Mac Cumhaill, is buried in the mound at Castleknock.

There were many struggles and battles in that immediate area, including contests between kings competing for the High Kingship of Ireland, Rory O'Connor's defeat by the Anglo Normans, and the various sieges of the castle by Edward the Bruce, Owen Roe O'Neill, General Monck and others.

In my research of the Barony of Castleknock I was helped by the fact that I have already researched and written two editions of a local history of the area, entitled *A Candle in the Window*. I was reared close to the area in Cabra and I have been living in Carpenterstown for the past 30 years. My grandfather, James Lacey, was baptised in St Brigid's Blanchardstown in 1862 and my grandmother, Rosanna Hanlon from Dunsink, was also baptised in St Brigid's. Her family, the Hanlons, may have been living in the area from the late 1600s. My father, who was reared in Ashtown, was a great storyteller and seemed to know nearly everybody in the area. He had a keen interest in the local history and passed that interest on to me.

I am a member of Blanchardstown/Castleknock History Society. The society does much to promote the study and enjoyment of the history of the local area. My fellow members were generous to me in giving me assistance and encouragement while I was writing this book.

When I had completed the research for my second edition of *A Candle in the Window*, in my foolishness I thought there was little history left to be uncovered. I soon discovered that I had been only peering through a keyhole and even at this stage of my study I have only prised open the door to just glimpse the past. Others are already assisting in opening this door further and more will follow.

This book has lots of new information, particularly relating to the many big demesnes that are a feature of the area. Part of the story relates to the families that lived in those demesnes and the people who worked for them. Many of the demesne owners were titled people; some held high positions in the British military or sat in the Westminster parliament, some were involved in world affairs and others were involved in literature, theatre and the arts.

I want in this book to take readers on a journey so they can picture the people and the places and enter into the houses and fields and workplaces and meet them and see how they lived, worked and played. Sometimes we will see how they suffered and in certain instances how they caused others to suffer.

The book will speak of achievements, of failures, of war, of peace, of love, of hate, of triumph and of disaster but mostly it will celebrate the lives of those that lived here before us. Those folk worked and toiled and did much to create the idyllic woodlands, pastures, parks and villages that we enjoy today.

For instance, the Guinness brewing family are associated with Farmleigh, Knockmaroon and Luttrellstown estates. The Churchill family lived for a while in the Phoenix Park, as did various Irish presidents and British viceroys and chief secretaries. A number of those chief secretaries went on to hold senior Cabinet positions, indeed some became prime ministers.

The Luttrells of Luttrellstown lived there for almost 600 years and had a significant influence on the politics and government of Great Britain as well as Ireland. Like many families, they had a few black sheep. Unfortunately the bad ones were so bad that they are the ones who are remembered and the deeds of the decent ones have been forgotten.

Many distinguished churchmen lived in the area. Two Roman Catholic Archbishops of Dublin were born in houses at opposite ends of one field, one in 1695 and the other in 1739. It's now a playing pitch but it is still called the Bishop's Field to this day.

The area lays claim to having one of the oldest brass bands in the country – the Blanchardstown Brass Band, founded in 1826, which is still providing great musical entertainment both locally and nationally.

The Phoenix Park was enclosed in 1663-1664 and is the largest enclosed public park in Europe. Phoenix Park is home to the oldest cricket club in Ireland, Phoenix Cricket Club, which was founded in 1830. Dublin Zoo, across the road from the cricket club, opened its gates one year later, making it one of the oldest zoos in the world. The All-Ireland Polo Club, based on the 'Nine Acres' in the Phoenix Park, is reputed to be the oldest polo club in the world, having being founded in 1873.

Blanchardstown Shopping Centre is the largest shopping centre in Ireland, while Blanchardstown village and its urban area is the largest urban area in Fingal County.

Castleknock and its surroundings were noted worldwide for the breeding and training of bloodstock. Many racehorses born and trained in the area won Grand Nationals, Derbies and other British and Irish Classic Races.

I have enjoyed gathering the images and researching and writing the history of this beautiful and fascinating area of County Dublin and I do hope you take as much enjoyment in perusing the pictures and reading the story of the Barony of Castleknock.

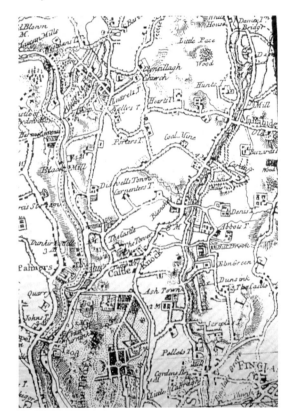

An extract of John Rocque's Map of County Dublin, 1760, showing the Barony of Castleknock. John (Jean) Rocque was born in France around 1704. His family were French Huguenot immigrants who had left their homeland owing to religious persecution. He was a surveyor and cartographer and for a time was involved in landscaping gardens for some of the great houses.

His map of London, published in 1737, took 10 years to produce and consisted of twenty-four printed sheets. He also published maps of other English and Welsh counties.

In 1756 he mapped Dublin City and in 1760 he published maps of County Dublin on four sheets. He also produced maps of Cork City, Kilkenny City and County Armagh.

The details of his maps were extraordinary and are not unlike aerial photographs, showing houses, hedgerows and trees. His maps are the earliest example of detailed mapping in Ireland and can measure up to modern standards of cartography.

The Sandpit Cottages Diswellstown, by Eugene Kennedy. These rustic estate cottages, placed in a delightful woodland setting and with their distinctive blue and white colours, are much commented on by visitors to the locality. They date back to the mid-nineteenth century and were built for workers on the Guinness estate. They have featured in motion pictures filmed in the locality, including BBC1's the *Inspector George Gently* series.

Castleknock Castle, 1698. This painting by Eugene Kennedy is after a contemporary drawing by Francis Place with the permission of Mr John Maher and courtesy of the late Fr John Doyle CM.

The artist Francis Place (1647-1728) was a native of Yorkshire and on a visit to Leinster he made sketches of the locations he visited. The castle, dating back to about 1205, was built on a hill 60 feet high. The undulating configuration of the hill had to be taken into consideration in the design of the castle, hence its multiangled, irregular appearance. It withstood many battles and sieges well, including bombardment by cannon. Some of its building blocks were sold off to Luke Gardiner and recycled for use in the building of his Mountjoy House in nearby Phoenix Park.

1

ABBOTSTOWN & DUNSINK, INCLUDING CAEVEEN GRAVEYARD

Lord Holmpatrick's estate at Abbotstown was immediately adjacent to Blanchardstown village and the townland of Abbotstown consisted almost entirely of Lord Holmpatrick's demesne. The old cemetery of Caeveen can be accessed through the National Sports Campus with permission.

Dunsink Observatory is well worth a visit and there are open nights during the winter months when the heavens can be viewed through the telescope.

The townlands of Abbotstown and Dunsink are now bisected by the M50 motorway; however, they still retain some of their rural character.

Sir Frederick John Falkiner was 1st Baronet Falkiner of Abbotstown 1768-1824 and was a son of Daniel Falkiner who was Lord Mayor of Dublin 1739-1740 and MP for Baltinglass 1727-1759 in the Irish House of Commons. Sir Frederick Falkiner followed his father into parliament, being elected MP for Athy in the Irish House of Commons 1791-1798 and thereafter for Dublin County until the Act of Union in 1801. Following the Act of Union, he sat as MP in the Westminster Parliament for Dublin County until 1807. He represented Carlow in Westminster from 1808 until 1812 and was created a baronet in 1812. He was also High Sheriff of Dublin from 1801-1802. He was totally opposed to the Act of Union and resisted all bribes and favours to change his vote.

He raised and equipped an infantry regiment – the 100th Regiment of Foot in 1804. Two years later, while sailing to Canada the regiment, numbering 560 men, were caught up in a fierce storm. The ship foundered and 192 men drowned. Falkiner was devastated and did his best to look after the relatives of those who were lost at sea. This financial burden, as well as the raising of the regiment, compromised his finances and he died tragically in Naples in 1824.

The regiment was granted the title of HRH the Prince Regent's County Dublin Regiment of Foot. It eventually merged into the Leinster Regiment until its disbandment in 1922. The Leinster Regiment was based in Crinkle, Birr, County Offaly and won four Victoria Crosses in the First World War.

James Hamilton of Sheephill (1727-1800), painting (after) Gilbert Stuart, c. 1770. James Hans Hamilton reputedly fathered thirty-six children and married three times. In those years even the children of wealthy parents were victims of various childhood diseases so many may not have survived infancy.

An aunt of James Hamilton's, Elizabeth, married Fredrick Falkiner (not to be confused with their grandson Fredrick John Falkiner 1768-1782). The Hamiltons eventually purchased the estate of Abbotstown from their cousins and neighbours the Falkiners in 1832.

James Hamilton's son Hans was a captain in the 5th Royal Dragoons and was MP for County Dublin and was High Sheriff of Dublin in 1803, taking over the office from his cousin Fredrick John Falkiner.

James Hans Hamilton, son of James Hamilton, was MP for Dublin County from 1841 to 1863 and Deputy Lieutenant for the county and was High Sheriff in 1832. His son, Ion Trant Hamilton, married Lady Victoria Alexandrina Wellesley, granddaughter of the Duke of Wellington. He was MP for County Dublin from 1863 to 1865 and was invested as a Privy Councillor in 1887. He was created 1st Baron of Holmpatrick in 1897.

Hans Wellesley Hamilton, 2nd Baron Holmpatrick, photograph by Lafayette Dublin as pictured in *The Sketch*, 1898. Hans Wellesley Hamilton is 12 years of age in the photograph, having succeeded to the title of 2nd Baron Holmpatrick on his father's death. His father Ion Trant had only been elevated to the title the previous year and was 58 when he died.

Lord Holmpatrick, Baden-Powell and the Earl of Fingall, London, 1920, courtesy Fingal County Council. The occasion pictured is the 1st Scout World Jamboree in London 1920. The trio to the front of the picture inspecting the scouts are, from left to right: Lt Gen. Baden-Powell, the founder of the scouting movement; Hans Wellesley Hamilton, 2nd Baron Holmpatrick; and Arthur James Francis Plunkett, 11th Earl of Fingall.

Hans Wellesley Hamilton married Lady Edina Dorothy Hope Conyngham, daughter of the 4th Marquess Conyngham of Slane Castle. He pursued a military career and achieved the rank of captain in the 16th Lancers. He was awarded the Military Cross and Distinguished Service Order and fought in the First World War, where he was wounded. He was promoted to the rank of General Staff Officer in 1917. He helped found the Irish Hospital Sweepstakes, was on the board of Sir Patrick Dunn's Hospital and was a patron of the scouting movement. He also assisted his neighbour, Judge Wylie of Clonsilla House, in setting up the Irish Army Equitation School and served in the reserve force of the Irish Army at the outbreak of the Second World War. He was universally liked in the locality and was active in supporting local causes such as the Church of Ireland and St Brigid's Brass Band. He died in 1942.

Abbotstown House, 2013, photograph by Andrew Lacey. According to Francis E. Ball, the house was built in or about 1800 by James Hamilton, on a site north of the original Falkiner family home. The house has been much added to since then. The original house was the part of the house you see to the left of the picture surmounted with two chimneys. There appears to have been at least three additional extensions to the existing core building, one in 1868 and the last in or about the 1930s.

The National Sports Campus Authority carried out remedial work to the roof and plans are in hand to restore it to reflect its former glory. It had been altered to cater for offices and laboratory rooms during its use by the Department of Agriculture. As of now, the lands of the estate are being transformed into a vast complex designed to cater for many sports organisations.

Abbotstown House, from a photograph by Thomas Mason, c. 1919. The lands of Abbotstown are named after a family of Norman settlers of that name who left no records or trace of their sojourn here other than their name. In or about the year 1400 the lands were owned by Thomas Sergeant who was married to Joan Tyrrell, a sister of the 8th and last baron of Castleknock. When the Down Survey was taken, 'Sir John Dungan Irish Papist and Ignatius Mapus Protestant each held about 66 acres'. The old chapel of Caeveen is listed in the survey also.

Following the Restoration, a family named Long lived there, followed by one Richard Hanlon who is listed on King James's Army List. The Sweetman family from Kilkenny lived in that area towards the end of the seventeenth century. They joined with their neighbours, the Warrens of Corduff, in supporting Bonnie Prince Charlie in the 1745 Jacobite Rising. The Clements family later came to live here before they moved to Phoenix Park.

There Nathaniel Clements became Chief Ranger and occupied the house that later became the Viceregal Lodge and following that Áras an Uachtaráin, home of our President. The Falkiners and the Hamiltons whom we met earlier followed the Clements. The Falkiners and Hamiltons later intermarried and their descendants are the present holders of the Baronetcy of Holmpatrick.

Connolly Hospital, courtesy Helen Giblin Architect, A&D Wejchart & Partners, compliments Deborah Burke. Connolly Hospital now occupies a large part of the lands that made up the Holmpatrick's Abbotstown Estate. The Holmpatrick family, like many landowners, were subject to enormous death duties following Hans Wellesley Hamilton's death in 1942. His son James Hans Hamilton, 3rd Baron Holmpatrick, then aged just 15, was confronted with the reality of maintaining a large estate.

The State purchased 240 acres of Abbotstown's lands in 1947 to provide a 520-bed sanatorium for the treatment of patients with tuberculosis; this project was driven by Dr Noël Browne, the Minister for Health. The remaining 434 acres were sold to the Department of Agriculture in 1950 and now form the National Sports Campus.

James Hans Hamilton, the 3rd Baron died in 1991 and Hans James Hamilton, the 4th Baron Holmpatrick, the present holder of the title, lives in Cornwall.

James Connolly Memorial at Connolly Hospital, courtesy Ray Bateson from his book *Memorials of the Easter Rising*. James Connolly, the Labour Leader and 1916 Commandant General, was a great champion of the poor and underprivileged. Dr Noël Browne, the Minister for Health who had been instrumental in the building of the regional sanatorium, was a disciple of Connolly. Browne resigned from office in 1951 as a result of a controversy concerning the Mother and Child Health Scheme.

In the next Dáil, Browne sat as a Fianna Fáil TD, having resigned form Clann na Poblachta. He requested that Jim Ryan, the incoming Minister for Health, would arrange for the sanatorium to be named after Connolly. Ryan had attended Connolly when he was a medic in the Irish Volunteers in the GPO during the Rising so was delighted to agree.

The sanatorium was opened in 1955 and was blessed by the parish priest of Blanchardstown, Fr Curley, as Archbishop McQuaid refused to bless it owing to the association with James Connolly's name.

The sanatorium was designated as a general hospital in 1973 as the use of antibiotics had greatly reduced the incidence of tuberculosis.

Connolly Hospital is today a major teaching hospital with 394 beds. It serves a population of 333,100 people in West Dublin, Meath and Kildare.

Caeveen graveyard tombstones, photograph by Andrew Lacey. This photograph captures the sombre, forlorn atmosphere of this ancient burial ground. Its chapel is documented in the Down Survey as forming part of the lands of Abbotstown in the year 1641: 'There is upon the premises one Thatche house with several Cottages vallewed by the Jury att ffifteen pounds & The wall of an olde Chapple.' If the chapel was a ruin in 1641 we can assume it is of great antiquity.

The graveyard was on the crest of a hill on Dunsink Lane, at a sharp bend on the road. Dunsink Lane ran from Bockey's Bridge, which crossed the Tolka from River Road. It went up hill and turned sharply and continued on past Dunsink Observatory to join the Ratoath Road at Cappagh.

In 1996 Dunsink Lane was bisected by the new M50 motorway. Although it was initially re-joined with a new section of road it was later blocked off and it is no longer possible to use this route between Blanchardstown and Finglas.

Caeveen Chapel, photograph by Andrew Lacey. Beneath the clinging ivy and rampant vegetation is the only remaining wall of the chapel of Caeveen or Caoimhín, or Kevin in English. It appears that the chapel and burial ground may be pre-Norman as it was not the practice of the Anglo-Normans to name churches after Celtic saints such as St Kevin of Glendalough.

One historian made a case for *reilig Aeda Finn* being the source of the name. It translates as 'the grave of fair Hugh'. The argument is made that the 'g' *in reilig* was retained and the name was over time corrupted into 'Gaeveen' and eventually Caeveen. There is a poem in the Book of Leinster that refers to 'Reilíg Aeda Finn'. Nice as this theory is, I think it's too complicated to be true and usually the simple explanation is the best so I believe the chapel is dedicated to Naomh Caoimhín.

Many people believe that Archbishop Troy is buried in Caeveen; however, he lies in St Mary's Pro-Cathedral in Marlborough Street. The tomb of the Troy family is here and his brother Walter was buried here.

Caeveen graveyard, photograph by Andrew Lacey. This photograph shows how overgrown the graveyard has become in the seventeen years since the motorway works left it in eerie isolation. Standing on the long-disused roadway, the old tarmacadam is visible underneath the briars and brambles. If one looks downhill towards the River Tolka, to the point where Bockey's Bridge once spanned it, the road emerges from the gloom of the choking undergrowth and then disappears, back into the dank leafy depths of weeds and briars, on a journey to nowhere.

Caeveen graveyard at Dunsink Lane, c. 2007, photographer unknown. When this picture was taken nature had not reclaimed this old road and the graveyard was not overgrown. As I write in 2014 the road is covered in briars and brambles and the graveyard is in a similar state. This sweeping bend brought the road from Bockey's Bridge to Dunsink Observatory and on to the Ratoath road near Cappagh.

Bockey's Bridge at Abbotstown on what is now the present site of the National Sports Campus, photographer unknown, courtesy Fingal County Council. This bridge was dismantled and its granite blocks were numbered and stored in or about 1997. It was one of the finest bridges over the Tolka. The origin of the name Bockey's Bridge is unknown.

Dunsink Observatory, picture from *Dublin Penny Journal*, 1835. This print shows workers using scythes to mow the lawns of Dunsink Observatory's fine gardens. In the background, a gentleman in a stovepipe hat is accompanied by a lady in late Georgian dress.

The observatory was built in 1785 from an endowment received from Francis Andrews, provost of Trinity College. The location was selected because of the height of Dunsink Hill and its proximity to Dublin, yet still being far enough away from the then smog-laden city. The Revd Henry Usher, a most learned astronomer, was its first director. The poet William Wordsworth made several visits there and commented on its wonderful gardens.

Dunsink Observatory house and offices, 1998, photograph by Brendan Campion. The work carried out in Dunsink was not all about searching the heavens and gazing into the telescope. Much of the work is of a mathematical nature and involves the study of physics as well as astronomy.

From 1880 up to 1916 the official time in Ireland was defined as Dunsink time, 25 minutes and 21 seconds behind Greenwich Mean Time. In 1916 we adopted Greenwich Mean Time for Ireland.

Open nights are held on the first and third Wednesdays of each month during winter and one can view the heavens through the Grubb 12in (30cm) refracting telescope.

The Telescope Building Dunsink, 1998, photograph by Brendan Campion. This building houses the Grubb 30cm telescope, also known as the south telescope after Sir James South, who donated the lens. The domed roof of the building opens and turns 360° on its axis to allow a full view of the night sky.

The Grubb telescope was completed by Thomas Grubb of Rathmines in 1868. It replaced one made in the 1830s. Grubbs were famous worldwide for the quality of their work and when the telescope was renovated in 1987 only two parts had to be replaced owing to wear and tear and two other missing parts needed to be procured and fitted.

Sir William Rowan Hamilton, Dunsink Observatory's most noted director, painting unattributed. William Rowan Hamilton was born in Dublin in 1805 and became Professor of Astronomy at Dunsink in 1827. He was a child prodigy and had a particular ability with languages. He understood Hebrew at about seven years of age, along with Greek and Latin. By the age of 13 he had a working knowledge of Persian and Syriac. He went on to learn Arabic, Hindustani, Sanskrit, Malaysian and Marathi. In 1843 while strolling with his wife along the Royal Canal near Broombridge (Brougham Bridge) in a mental flash of inspiration he discovered quaternions. He carved the equation $i^2=j^2=k^2=ijk=-1$ into the stone of the bridge. His discovery is used today in computer graphics, spacecraft instrumentation and many other applications that could not have been realised without Hamilton's flash of inspiration. He also solved many other mathematical problems and he is one of our greatest scientists.

2

ASHTOWN, DUNSINEA & SCRIBBLESTOWN

Ashtown was quite a small village with a small population; however, the nearby candle factory and the oil mills and later the tin-box factory and the glove factory gave a lot of employment to people around the area, particularly those from Blackhorse Lane. Incidentally, Blackhorse Lane is now named Blackhorse Avenue but old locals still remember it as 'The Lane'.

A lot of people from the area were employed in the Phoenix Park and in the 'big' houses within the park as gardeners, domestic servants and grooms and coachmen. The Phoenix Park Racecourse and the various horse breeders and trainers located around the area also gave much employment.

The handball alley at the rear of the Halfway House was the scene of some thrilling competitions when Irish and provincial finals were contested with great vigour. The local football team, Elm Rovers, drew much support from the local area.

Ashtown Cross, Aerial View, c. 1948, photographer unknown. This picture displays a wonderful panoramic view of Ashtown when it was still a small rural hamlet. The large house on the bottom right foreground is Belleville – one time home to the Hendron family who had a machine and tool business in Broadstone. On the right is Kelly's Halfway House, a well-known pub and restaurant, still carrying the Kelly name from Giles Kelly and his father Peter but under the ownership now of Con Tracey. To the left of Kelly's is a small green with the Martin Savage Memorial in the centre; it was later moved to its present location. Set back behind the green is Ashtown Tin Box factory, built in 1925 but alas no longer in business. It was also known as the St Eloi Works (St Eloi is the patron saint of tinsmiths).

Behind that is George Horne's glove factory, built in 1945 but no longer trading. The grey building in the centre is Ashtown Oil Mills.

In the background, beyond is the wooded area surrounding Ashton House is the old Rathbornes candle factory with Dunsink Observatory in the distance.

The Empress Elisabeth's Mounting Platform at Ashtown Gate, 1998, photograph by Eugene Kennedy. This picture shows the author at the mounting platform constructed for the Austrian Empress to enable her to easily mount and dismount when riding her horses in Phoenix Park. Bellville House in the background and its lands were sold in or about 1999/2000 for private housing development. The mounting platform was accidentally destroyed at that time.

HM King Edward VII at the Phoenix Park Races in 1903, courtesy Fingal County Council. The Phoenix Park Racecourse opened in 1902 and was originally used for both steeplechasing and flat racing. The big race of the year was the 1,500 Guineas. It permanently closed for racing in 1990 and is now a housing development of fine apartments.

The picture shows, from left to right: the Duke of Devonshire, the Marquis of Londonderry, HRH the Duke of Connaught, HM King Edward VII. The Lord Lieutenant William Ward, 2nd Earl of Dudley, stands further away to the right, looking towards the King.

Timothy Healy, Governor General, and Lady Arnott at the Phoenix Park Races, 1920s, photographer Joseph Cashman, courtesy RTÉ Stills Library. Lady Arnott was the wife of Sir John Arnott, one of the founders of the Phoenix Park Racecourse.

Tim Healy played an important part in Irish politics throughout his life. In 1890 he had challenged Parnell about his relationship with Catherine O'Shea, which was causing tremendous controversy and affecting support for the party. The Irish Party split and Parnell, once known as the 'Uncrowned King of Ireland', became the 'Lost Leader'. Healy later became Governor General in the new Irish Free State. Some sources suggested that he was in fact a British Government agent who had been reporting to the British Intelligence Service since the Phoenix Park murders in 1882.

His nephew, Kevin O'Higgins, became Minister for Justice in the Irish Free State and Vice President of the Executive Council but was assassinated in 1927.

Jack Doyle with his wife Movita and Miss O'Keefe at the Phoenix Park Races in the 1940s, photographer Joseph Cashman, courtesy RTÉ Stills Library. Jack Doyle was a boxer, an actor and a singer known as the 'Gorgeous Gael'. He was a larger-than-life character and was much loved. The couple were very good looking and seemed to be made for each other but their love life was fairly tempestuous.

It was said that Doyle was not very skilled as a boxer and lacked discipline and drive but he had a good punch and won ten professional bouts in sequence, involving only fifteen rounds in total. Doyle had a drink problem and was a womaniser – he could not get enough of either. He turned to acting but his career never really took off. He died in 1978.

Movita broke up with Doyle and married Marlon Brando in 1960 but they divorced within two years.

Ashtown House, Phoenix Park Racecourse, courtesy Olivia Leonard of 'The Past and Present Blanchardstown & Surrounding Areas,' Online History Group. Harry Peard, son of John H.H. Peard, a veterinarian by profession and a founder of the Phoenix Park Club, was appointed secretary of the course in 1910. The Peard's Ashtown House was a fine Tudor-style house and was much admired by visitors. Following Harry's death his wife Frances took over the management of the course until her retirement in 1969.

Sir John Arnott 3rd Bt., son of another founder Sir John Alexander Arnott 2nd Bt., moved into Ashtown House until his death in 1981 and managed the racecourse during his time there. Sir John was of the Arnott drapery family and was a brother of the great horse trainer Maxie Arnott who had his stud farm in Clonsilla.

The racecourse closed in 1990 and is now the site of well-appointed apartments. However, the beautiful Tudor-style Ashtown House was burnt in 1999 and only the shell remains.

Frances Peard of Phoenix Park Racecourse in Local Security Force uniform, c. 1942, courtesy Elizabeth Reid. Frances Peard served in the Local Security Forces during the Second World War or, as we in Ireland called it, The Emergency. During that time Ireland remained neutral.

On a winter's night in 1942 a plane landed on the Phoenix Park Racecourse. Frances Peard, who was living there at the time, I am told, became aware of the stuttering mechanical sound of an aircraft in difficulty overhead. She promptly donned her military uniform and grabbed her own shotgun and was just in time to capture the pilot as he was exiting from the crashed aircraft.

The military authorities were summoned and the plucky Frances handed over her prisoner, an American Air Force pilot. The aircraft was seized and the pilot was interned in the Curragh for a couple of weeks until a conveniently open gate allowed him to make his way across the border where he re-joined his forces.

As far as I can gather, Frances Peard was the only lady apart from the nursing staff to serve in the Defence Forces at that time.

Rolling wax candles at Rathbornes Candles factory, c. 1896, courtesy John G. Rathborne, compliments Robbie Kelly. Rathbornes Candles factory is Ireland's oldest firm. Starting off in the Dublin Liberties in 1488, it moved to various different locations in its 500-plus years, arriving in Dunsinea, near Ashtown, in 1764.

The Candle Factory by Bernard Neary, published by Lilliput Press in 1998, gives the definitive history of the company. It survived wars, famine, fires and even a payroll robbery. The robbery occurred in 1923 and involved three thieves, of which two were serving soldiers in the National Army. Staff, incensed at their wages being snatched, pursued the robbers on bicycles and the police picked up their trail. The author's Uncle James was one of the pursuers. There was an exchange of shots between the CID men and the raiders and Det. Thomas Fitzgerald was shot dead. One of the raiders, William Downes, was hanged for the crime. He was the first person to be executed by hanging in the Free State.

In 1925 Rathbornes moved their candle factory from Dunsinea to their East Wall storage depot but in 2002 they moved back to this area of Dublin – this time to Rosemount Business Park, Blanchardstown.

Master wax chandlers at Rathborne's Candles factory, courtesy John G. Rathborne, compliments Robbie Kelly. Candle makers were known officially as chandlers but everyone called them waxies because of the wax used in candle making. The popular Dublin ballad 'The Waxies Dargle' refers to the work outings to the popular scenic spot the Dargle Valley, near Bray.

Before statutory holidays were introduced the work outing or beano was the highlight of the year. It involved a trip to a local resort, a picnic, a few drinks and a singsong.

Candle making was an art and master chandlers were valued workers.

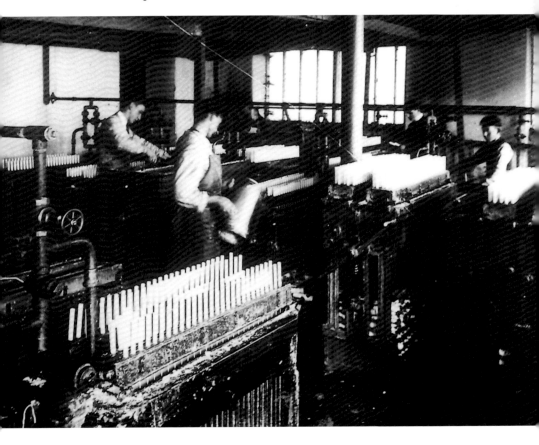

Cast-iron statue of a lock-keeper on the Royal Canal, Ashtown, photograph by Andrew Lacey. The lock-keeper's job was a busy one when the canals were full of barges pulled by horses and in later times when motorised barges plied back and forth. The Royal Canal was built between 1790 and 1817. However, the building of the railway, commencing in 1846, heralded the canal's demise. The canal finally closed to commercial traffic in 1955.

My great-grandfather, Denis Lacey, and a grand-uncle, another Denis Lacey, were lock-keepers at the tenth lock Ashtown from about 1848 up till the mid-1920s. My great-grandfather told my father that he recalled seeing the workers laying down the new railway. In or about 1890, while closing the lock gates one frosty night, one of my great-aunts slipped on the icy stones and ended up in the lock chamber. The voluminous dresses then worn by ladies saved her life; the buoyancy created by the trapped air in her skirts lasted long enough for her to be fished out with a barge pole.

Ashtown Oil Mills in 1998, photograph by author. This mill was built around 1820 and was owned by the McGarry family. Bernard McGarry donated the church bell for St Brigid's church, Blanchardstown, in 1852. The mill was sold at auction to McMaster Hodgson in 1863. The mill was used to manufacture products from linseed oil, a by-product of the process of processing flax into linen. Linseed was used to produce cow cakes, linseed oil, polish and various other oils. The Ronuk Company later used it to manufacture floor polish. The hair oil brilliantine was also connected with the mill as large quantities of the distinctive long narrow bottles were discovered there when it fell into ruin. The Rathbornes also leased part of the mill for a period after the 1895 fire at their Dunsinea premises. The beautiful copper-faced clock (see picture), with its blue-green face, was a landmark visible for miles around. It was believed to have come from Newgate Gaol in Dublin. Unfortunately it was stolen during the Christmas period of 2012.

James Lacey & Rosanna Hanlon, 1898. The photograph depicts the author's grandparents on their wedding day. My grandfather was a millwright in Ashtown Mill and was politically active in the old Nationalist Party at local level. My grandmother came from a small dairy farm on Dunsink Lane and worked as a parlour maid in nearby Ashton House, home to the Levins-Moore family. Both were baptised St Brigid's church in Blanchardstown, my grandfather in 1862 and my grandmother in 1874. He died of 'Spanish Flu' in 1918 and she lived on until 1944.

Bridge at Ashtown over Tolka River, c. 1910, courtesy Fingal County Council. This bridge crosses the Tolka River on the road to Dunsinea and Scribblestown. The Tolka is an unpredictable river and prone to flooding. In fact, the river's original Irish name, *An Tulcha*, means flood. I have seen this bridge with the debris of trees and bushes piled to the keystone after heavy rains.

The Tolka has recovered after years of neglect and is now stocked again with trout. Recent reports from Inland Fisheries in 2011 confirm that wild Atlantic salmon have also been reproducing in the river.

Unfortunately a significant fish kill occurred in July 2014 when an unknown pollutant entered the water near Finglas Bridge. As I write, investigations are still on-going.

Dunsinea Manor, photographer unknown. This fine house was once home to the Rathborne family of candle-making fame. Henry Rathborne married Jane Bayly from Nenagh, County Tipperary. Jane's sister Helen met William Rowan Hamilton, their neighbour and the director of the nearby Dunsink Observatory, while visiting her sister. They eventually married. It was Helen who was walking beside William Rowan Hamilton at Broombridge on the Royal Canal on the momentous day that he discovered the formula for quaternion multiplication.

The house is in the townland of Scribblestown but the Rathbornes are believed to have dreamt up the name Dunsinea. There is an old right of way across the lands linking Dunsink to the River Road. It is used once a year in October when mathematicians and historians retrace Hamilton's fortuitous walk to Broombridge.

Walton's famous music shop on North Frederick Street, courtesy Patrick Walton. Martin Walton set up the Dublin College of Music and a retail music business here in 1924. Later on they manufactured musical instruments and published classic collections of Irish music and booklets of Irish songs. In 1952 he started to manufacture records under the label Glenside.

The *Walton's Radio Programme* on Saturday afternoons was eagerly listened to each week by a massive audience. The listeners were urged by presenter Leo Maguire, 'If you feel like singing, do sing an Irish song'. Martin Walton lived in Ashtown Lodge on River Road. He was a veteran of the 1916 Rising and was interned in Balykinlar Camp. While there, he set up an orchestra with his fellow inmates. He founded his music business six years later.

Martin Walton died in May 1981, aged 80, but was still active and involved in his music business up to his death. Martin Walton's contribution to Irish music, song and poetry was truly monumental.

The Waltons have opened a new shop in Blanchardstown Shopping Centre.

Ashton House, Ashtown, courtesy Fingal County Council. Ashton House appears to have been built in the early to mid-nineteenth century. The house was enlarged and remodelled in 1891 and this work is attributed to William Hague.

Andrew Thomas Moore, born 1821, was the first owner. He was a part-owner of the McArdle-Moore brewing company. His wife, Anne Mary Levins, was one of the Levins family from County Louth. Their son, Tom Levins-Moore, was born in 1871. He married Florence Smithwick of the well-known Kilkenny brewing family. He was a barrister and a Justice of the Peace. Tom's sister Mary married Thomas P. Martin of the famed timber-importing firm. Their daughter, Marie, was the founder of the Medical Missionaries of Mary.

Kevin McClory, the famous film producer and director, lived in Ashton House in the 1960s. He was born in Dublin and was related to the Brontë sisters.

Scene of the Ashtown Ambush of December 1919, photographer unknown. On 19 December 1919, a unit of the Dublin Brigade of the Irish Republican Army under the command of Paddy Daly ambushed the Lord Lieutenant and a contingent of the British Army at Ashtown Cross. The Lord Lieutenant Lord French escaped without injury but some of his party were wounded. Martin Savage, one of attacking party was fatally wounded; another, Dan Breen, was shot in the leg. A constable, Con O'Loughlin, was wounded in the foot and Det. Sgt Hally, who was in Lord French's car, was shot in the hand.

Some weeks later, Dan Breen met Maude Gonne McBride and Charlotte Despard in Grafton Street. Both ladies were die-hard republicans. Breen was taken aback when Madame Despard scolded him about the Ashtown Ambush and his attempts to murder her 'Johnnie'. Lord John French was Charlotte Despard's brother!

Lord John Denton Pinkstone French, 1st Earl of Ypres, photograph taken from an old cigarette card. Lord French was born in Kent and educated at Harrow. His family owned a large estate in Roscommon and he considered himself Irish but was politically Unionist. In direct contrast, his sister Charlotte was a doctrinaire Republican and supported Sinn Féin and the Irish Republican Army. She became a Catholic and at the same time struck up a friendship with Karl Marx's daughter Eleanor, leading her to eventually embrace communism. Despite being on opposite poles politically and socially, she and her brother Johnnie remained friends throughout the years.

Lord French had a mixed military career, starting off in the Royal Navy then joining the cavalry. He fought in the Sudan, India and South Africa and in 1914 he led the British Expeditionary Force where he was popular with his men. However, following several lost battles involving massive casualties, French was returned to England as Commander in Chief of British Home Forces and given a peerage. In May 1918 he was given the job of Lord Lieutenant of Ireland to achieve a military solution to the Irish problem. He saw himself as a 'Military Viceroy heading a Quasi-Military Administration'.

Lieutenant Martin Savage, Irish Republican Army, photograph courtesy irishvolunteers.org, compliments James Langton. Martin Savage was born in Ballisodare, County Sligo, in 1898 and fought in the Easter Rising when only 17 years of age. He was acting as a brigade quartermaster in 1919 and it was not originally intended that he would be deployed for the Ashtown Ambush. However, when he heard from Dan Breen and Sean Hogan about the intended operation he insisted on participating.

During the exchange of fire Martin Savage was shot in the neck and died almost instantly. A memorial was erected to him at Ashtown crossroads, in 1948.

Blackhorse Tavern or 'The Hole in the Wall', photograph Lawrence Collection, courtesy National Library of Ireland. This image dates back to about 1907, when Levinus Doyle owned the pub. A previous owner, Nancy Hand, was well known for the 'party atmosphere' enjoyed during her tenancy.

The pub dates back to the mid-1600s and the lane was called Blackhorse Lane because of the tavern's name.

During the First World War the adjacent Phoenix Park was used by the British Army to hold troops awaiting embarkation to the front lines. In 1917/1918 over 40,000 troops were living under canvas in the park. The turnstile in the park wall at the entrance to the pub gave rise to the nickname 'The Hole in the Wall', as in 'I'm going down to the hole in the wall for a pint'. The name stuck.

The Hole in the Wall, painting by Phil Parker, c. 1995, courtesy McCaffrey family. It shows the much-extended pub, now claimed to be the longest pub in Ireland. It is nowadays a very fine restaurant also.

One of the pub's visitors was Daniel O'Connell, the famous Irish advocate and parliamentarian. One of the many presidents who lived across the road in Áras an Uachtaráin was also known to nip in for a 'ball of malt'. Seán T. O'Kelly would on occasion drop in and have a read of the newspaper while lingering over a small whiskey. The locals never disturbed him and he enjoyed his privacy while having a quiet drink in a congenial atmosphere.

3

BLANCHARDSTOWN & MULHUDDART, INCLUDING CLOGHRAN & CORDUFF

Blanchardstown and Castleknock are the most prominent villages in the Barony of Castleknock. Blanchardstown is more commercialised than Castleknock, yet Castleknock had a bank before Blanchardstown – the penny bank that eventually evolved into the large commercial bank of Guinness and Mahon.

Blanchardstown takes its name from the Blanchard family who appear to have been granted their estate by Sir Richard Tyrrell, the 4th Baron of Castleknock. The names Blanchard and Plunkett are derived from the Norman-French word *blanch*, meaning pale or white. We use the same word today when we blanch vegetables in cooking or, for example, earthing up celery in the garden to prevent the sunlight reaching their lower stems, causing them to blanch. In the case of the name Blanchard, it may refer to the colour of a person's skin or hair or maybe a tendency to turn white in battle. In any event, all we know of the Blanchards is they moved to Tipperary and no more was heard of them.

The Blanchards, the Diswells, the Pilates, the Le Hunts, the Carpenters and the Bossards gave their names to Blanchardstown, Diswellstown, Pelletstown, Huntstown, Carpenterstown and Bossardstown (now Buzzardstown). That was the Anglo-Norman way of identifying their claim to the land. The native Irish did not exercise as much proprietorial claim as the land was held by the clan and included much commonage and woodland.

The Castleknock Barony stretched from Cabra to Clonee and from the Liffey to what is today's North Road. It was mainly covered in dense woodland with only small areas cleared for settlement. The Norman settlers cleared swathes of forest and moved the system of farming from pasture to tillage. However, as late as 1652 the authorities had to take measures to curb the huge population of wolves in the Great Scaldwood of Blanchardstown. The amount of woodland required to support such a large population of wolves would have been considerable.

Over the centuries many armies passed through the area, sometimes leaving death and destruction behind. The Black Death visited the area and wiped out most of the Tyrrell family.

In the late 1700s new and better farming practices increased the yield of various crops and animal husbandry improved. Yet there were times of famine and want. Thankfully the Great Potato Famine did not affect the area badly as it did not have a big dependence on the potato crop.

The area had many mills owing to its proximity to the Liffey and the Tolka. There were also local industries such as flax mills and the candle factory. The land was fertile and the limestone-rich soil made it ideal for horse breeding.

The population was mainly Roman Catholic and had services in chapels attached to some of the big houses or at Mass rocks during the penal times. The register of baptisms in the area commenced during Fr Bermingham's time, with the first dated 1757.

Fr Talbot, who arrived in the parish in 1769, built a small chapel consisting of mud walls, a thatched roof and a dirt floor. It was located in the circle occupied by St Brigid's statue outside the present church.

The first Mass in the present church was celebrated on 29 October 1837. However, the steeple was not built until 1869. During the 1800s the parish of St Brigid's church included the modern parishes of Cabra, Navan Road, Chapelizod, Castleknock, Corduff, Clonsilla, Mulhuddart, Mountview, Blakestown, Huntstown and Hartstown.

Blanchardstown remained a small rural village until the early 1970s, with about 700 living in Blanchardstown village and the surrounding area, including Clonsilla and Mulhuddart. It has now expanded to become the largest urban area of Fingal County Council with a population of over 68,000 people.

The Blanchardstown Shopping Centre, which opened in 1996, has 180 stores with plans for further development. There is a nine-screen cinema, a leisure centre, a theatre and arts centre, a hotel and a very fine public library – the largest public library in Ireland.

The Institute of Technology Blanchardstown was founded in 1999, caters for over 2,500 students and covers a myriad of educational courses, including Social Studies, Business, Computing, Digital Media, Engineering, Horticulture, Languages, Social and Community Development, Sports Management, and Early Childhood Care and Education. Courses cover higher certificate, ordinary degree, honours degree and master degree levels.

Up until fifteen years ago the vast majority of people living in the Blanchardstown area were born in Ireland. In 2011 the census of population showed that 23.5 per cent of the population were non-Irish nationals; that is double the national average. The breakdown shows that 4,448 were from Poland, 5,678 were from other European Union countries and 9,393 from the rest of the world.

Blanchardstown has changed and will continue to change.

Main Street, Blanchardstown, 1909, photograph courtesy Fingal County Council. We can identify who lived in each house in the photograph from records and local memories: the first house after Church Avenue (then known as Chapel Lane) belonged to the Pattersons (later Mahers), then comes Doyle's Shop and St Brigid's Cottages. In the next cottages lived the Colemans, Bannertons, Doolans (later Andersons), Thomas Duffy and James Duffy. Then there was a laneway, followed by the O'Briens' house (later Millers), then the Stewarts, Sheridans, Smiths and, hidden behind the hedge, is the Lawlers' cottage. These names were gathered from the 1911 Census with the assistance of Marie Cummins, secretary of Blanchardstown & Castleknock History Society and a long-time resident of the area.

Maggie Doyle's Shop, c. 1995, photographer unknown. Doyle's shop opened for business in 1837. It opened at the same time as the new St Brigid's church and the Doyles, who were relatives of the previous owners, moved in about the late 1890s from nearby Ashtown. Doyle's premises originally had a thatched roof, as did many other houses in and around Blanchardstown.

It was no coincidence that Doyle's shop opened around the same time that the 'new' St Brigid's opened, nor was it a coincidence that it opened in the present location. Business follows people so where better to have a shop catering for most of our needs than beside a building where most of the population were required to attend Mass at least once a week?

After Mass on Sunday the shop would be packed with customers milling around for their weekly newspaper, groceries, tobacco and sweets for the kids. The shop was not only a purveyor of goods but also a place where information was exchanged. It was the usual tittle-tattle that keeps small communities going. The shop was a place where you could be made aware of the plight of some neighbours, of the good fortune of others or where you might be the recipient of consolation, congratulation and occasionally envy, as was appropriate.

There you would discover who was ill, who had passed away, who had lost a job or had other difficulties and help was always on hand. There would be talk of people emigrating, people getting married or engaged and of young people passing exams or getting new jobs. It was as much a community centre as a shop.

Local couple John and Annie Byrne on their wedding day, *c.* 1915, photographer unknown. Margaret Doyle (of Doyle's shop) is pictured on the left, followed by Ned Byrne and Agnes Hickey. John and Annie Byrne are seated. This picture first appeared in *Newswest Year Book* in 1995.

The girl in the white pinafore, Chapel Lane (later Church Avenue), 1914, courtesy Fingal County Council. It is an idyllic summer's scene – a fine sunlit day, a pram is parked on the lane, allowing the baby inside a little airing. A young girl wearing a white pinafore stands vigilant at her gate, minding the baby.

When meeting Joe McGregor, a long-time 'Blanchie', to discuss the identification of the personnel in the Blanchardstown Brass Band, I showed him this picture with a view to getting a date for the photograph. As it turned out, the girl in the white pinafore was Joe McGregor's mother, Kathleen Sullivan in 1914, then aged about 10.

St Brigid's church, Blanchardstown, 2011, photograph by author. St Brigid's church opened on 29 October 1837, when Fr Michael Dungan celebrated Mass there for the first time. The church was finally finished with the addition of a beautiful spire. It was erected in the year 1858 by Beardwood & Co. but the bell did not arrive for another four years. It is believed that the Flemish design was the inspiration of Fr Joseph Joy Deane, who had ministered in that part of Europe.

Fr Deane was a first cousin of Henry Joy McCracken, the leader of the 1798 Rebellion in Antrim. Fr Deane filled in for Fr McPharlan, who had to go into exile on the Isle of Man, and was officially appointed as parish priest in 1825. He was followed by Fr Michael Dungan, appointed in 1836 and in office until 1868.

During his years in Blanchardstown he recorded a remarkable diary of all the goings-on in the parish. Much of the diary relates to Church business but there are insights into the social life of the parish and anecdotes about farming practices and the triumphs and tragedies that affected the parish.

Fr Dungan was parish priest during the potato famine and although it was not very bad in Blanchardstown, there was hunger and disease. No deaths occurred in the area from hunger but many died from diseases associated with poor diet. Cholera was a particularly bad problem in the area.

St Brigid's Circle, St Brigid's church grounds, Blanchardstown, 2011, photograph by author. St Brigid's statue is set within a circular garden beside St Brigid's church. The circle, or 'The Ring' as it's called locally, marks the location of the original chapel dating back to 1769, when Fr Richard Talbot had it built. He was appointed that same year as parish priest by Dr Patrick Fitzsimons, Archbishop of Dublin.

Dr Fitzsimons himself hailed from the Blanchardstown area. He was born in Porterstown near the Royal Canal at Kennan's Bridge and is buried in St Mary's churchyard, Clonsilla.

When Fr Talbot built his chapel it could not be built of stone, have a steeple or bell and could not be located on a main road as the penal laws were still on the statute books. In fact, the parishioners would not have been able to fund a stone building with spires and bells so the penal laws made little difference. Besides, these laws were gradually being relaxed at this time.

The chapel would have been a mud wall building with a thatched roof and a clay floor and it served the parish well until 1837, when the present church was built.

The old Royal Irish Constabulary Barracks Blanchardstown, c. 1904, courtesy Fingal County Council. The four members of the local RIC are standing outside their barracks and appear at ease and relaxed. In the early 1900s the British administration had embarked on a policy of killing Home Rule with kindness. There was little or no agrarian trouble and few political disturbances.

The barracks would later be partly destroyed in the War of Independence. The use of the word 'barracks' gives a clue about the military nature of the RIC. Although none of the constables in the photograph appear to be armed, the building behind them would have several Lee-Enfield carbines and Webley revolvers and plenty of ammunition. The officers would be well trained in firearms practice.

The RIC was the eyes and ears of the government and rigorously enforced the laws, yet the constables were friendly, helpful and efficient and got on well with the people. This changed after 1916 and by 1920 there was such enmity between the Irish people and the Crown Forces that many of the rank and file had taken early retirement or had resigned.

Their replacement by temporary constables, i.e. the Black and Tans and the Auxiliary Division, and their indiscipline and misconduct was the death knell for the RIC.

The barracks was rebuilt after the 'Troubles' as a butcher's shop. Today the premises is shared by a firm of solicitors and a florist's shop.

In 1911 Sgt Francis Hendy and constables Joseph Fox and Michael Harrison and another constable whose name is lost were serving the people of Blanchardstown. Many RIC men joined An Garda Síochána when the new State was formed.

P. O'Reilly, victuallers, Blanchardstown, *c.* 1930, photograph courtesy Fingal County Council. The man in the butcher's smock on the left is Patrick O'Reilly, the founder of the business.

In those years it was common practice to have sides of beef and mutton hanging outside the windows of the shop. Many a time did I enjoy a nice piece of steak from this fine establishment. Patrick O'Reilly married Josephine Corcoran from Crevlin farm, Castleknock.

Josephine Corcoran and Ellen Corcoran, *née* Carr, pictured outside their home, Crevlin Farm, *c.* 1920s, courtesy Darach Corcoran. Ellen was the wife of Thomas Corcoran and Josephine was one of their daughters. They lived on Crevlin Farm near Granard Bridge on the Royal Canal. Thomas Corcoran named the farm after a place where a large bough of a tree hung over a small pond on his land: *Craobh* is Irish for a bough or a branch, and *linn* is a pool. Thus we arrive at the name *Craobh Linn*. It was anglicised as Crevlin but all the locals called it 'The Bridge Farm' because it was near the bridge. The Corcoran family also owned a bar and grocery. It was sold to Davy & Phelan and they, in turn, sold it on in the 1990s and today it is The Bell Public House, a popular local hostelry.

Blanchardstown railway station, c. 1920s, courtesy Fingal County Council. The station served both Castleknock and Blanchardstown but was in the townland of Castleknock. The new station at Laurel Lodge that replaced it is in the townland of Blanchardstown. The border between the townlands of Blanchardstown and Castleknock is defined by a small underground stream that crosses the road diagonally from just south of the entrance to Laurel Lodge to just north of Claremont on the opposite side of Castleknock Road, continuing on diagonally in the direction of the canal midway to a point halfway between Granard Bridge and Talbot Bridge and along the canal, meeting Abbotstown on the far side of the M50 roundabout. The stream rises in Carpenterstown townland and nowadays it is mostly underground.

Unfortunately the fine old railway station in the picture was destroyed in the works associated with the M50 motorway.

M.M. Donnelly's Pub, Talbot Bridge, Blanchardstown, c. 1940s, courtesy Fingal County Council. The pub was also called the Railway Bar as it was close to the entrance of Blanchardstown station. Before it became a pub it was an RIC barracks. It later became 'The Curtain Cottage' and then a bicycle shop. The owner transferred the licence to a new bar and lounge, the Twin Oaks, which then became the Castleknock Inn and later on it became Scotts' and then Brady's.

The Railway Bar featured in the motion picture *Young Cassidy*, starring Rod Taylor, Julie Christie and Maggie Smith. The film was based on the life of Sean O'Casey..

O'Brien's Shop, Mill Lane, courtesy Olivia Leonard, 'The Past & Present Blanchardstown & Surrounding Areas', Online History Group. The O'Brien family supplied Blanchardstown for years with milk from their own dairy on Mill Road. Jimmy 'Ducky' O'Brien delivered the milk and Jimmy's daughter Ciss ran the shop. Jimmy's son, another Jimmy, was an insurance agent and was a great Gaelic footballer in his day, a stalwart in St Brigid's GAA Club. He also played in the Blanchardstown Brass Band.

The Saluting Base Emergency Services Parade, Blanchardstown, 1943, courtesy Sheila Browne. When Germany invaded Poland and France and Britain declared war on Germany the world plunged into the catastrophe of the Second World War. While this war raged worldwide we in Ireland had 'The Emergency' and remained neutral. While we adopted that stance, we now know we were neutral in favour of the allies.

At the start of the war we had a tiny aircorps, virtually no navy and our army was understrength with poor equipment, a few artillery pieces, a few anti-aircraft guns and no modern tanks.

The government quickly launched a recruiting campaign and imported new military equipment. The much-strengthened army and reserves eventually numbered 200,000. Large-scale manoeuvres were conducted countrywide and the Blanchardstown area was selected for some of the strategic exercises as it could be a strongpoint where forces advancing from the north might be stopped just south of the line of the River Boyne. Similar exercises were conducted in Cork and Waterford along the line of the River Blackwater, should an invasion come from that direction.

In this picture Fr Michael Coogan, parish priest, is standing in the back row in clerical attire. The lady in the white trench coat is Frances Peard. The officer wearing the Sam Browne belt at front is Michael McCoy and the soldier at rear to left of McCoy is Ned Hughes.

Emergency Services Parade, Blanchardstown, 1943, courtesy Sheila Browne. The Blanchardstown Pipe Band lead the emergency parade and are followed by members of the Local Defence Force who were a reserve force for the Garda Síochána. The soldiers standing at 'slope arms' at the saluting base are members of the Local Defence Force. After the Emergency the LDF became the FCA or Fórsa Cosanta Áitiúil.

Blanchardstown post office, *c.* 1980, photograph courtesy Olivia Leonard, 'The Past and Present Blanchardstown and Surrounding Areas', Online History Group. In 1911 the Blanchardstown post office was in Main Street and the postmistress was Margaret Donohoe.

The post office here was probably photographed in the 1980s. Prior to that, the Irish name for Blanchardstown was given as *Baile Luindin* – in this photograph it appears on the front of the post office as *Baile Bhlainséir*. The Irish name *Baile Luindin* came about at a time when the State was attempting to gather proper Irish place names and current spellings for each townland. Various Gaelic scholars were given the task of translating these names into Irish. One of these scholars Seosamh O'Laoide was told by his mother that on her travels by coach from Navan to Dublin the last stage where horses were changed was *Baile Luindin*. So he put two and two together and got five because *Baile Luindin* is the Irish name for Blundellstown near Tara. Blanchardstown in fact never had an Irish name. It was a town or townland, an Anglo-Norman invention and therefore did not have an Irish name.

In the United States there is a suburb of Oklahoma called Blanchard and there are also towns in Louisiana, Idaho and North Dakota similarly named.

Incidentally, nearly all the locals in Blanchardstown drop the 'd' and pronounce it as Blancherstown.

Blanchardstown Brass Band, St Patrick's Day, 1942, courtesy John Harford, Blanchardstown Brass Band. The bandsmen are relaxing, having marched in the St Patrick's Day Parade in Blanchardstown, leading the Local Defence Force Unit through the village. One of the band members, Charlie Conlon, is still in uniform.

The Local Defence Force was a part-time reserve trained to provide a back-up to the Irish Army at this crucial time in the Second World War. Both Germany and Britain and her allies were anxious to secure the Irish ports for their own interests. The Irish Government had adapted a policy of neutrality and had pledged to defend its territory by force of arms. The Blanchardstown Brass Band leading the Local Defence Force in parade through the village while playing martial airs lifted morale and at the same time attracted young men to join up.

Back row, from left to right: Johnny Phelan, George Johnston, -?-, -?-, Paddy Buggy, John Larkin, Dessie Byrne. Front row: Larry Lynch, Jimmy O'Brien, -?-, Eddie Meehan, George Johnston Jnr, Charlie Conlon, ? Farmer. Thanks to Joe McGregor, his wife Kathleen and Marie Mulholland for assisting in the identification.

Blanchardstown Brass Band in their new uniforms, 1959, courtesy John Harford, Blanchardstown Brass Band. The band were participating at the unveiling of a monument in Ashbourne to commemorate the Battle of Ashbourne in 1916 when the Irish Volunteers routed superior Royal Irish Constabulary forces.

The band became aware that they alone of all the participants in the commemoration were in civilian dress. A decision was therefore made at the next meeting to acquire smart new uniforms. The uniforms consisted of navy blue jackets and slacks with light blue piping on the sleeves. A navy cap with a white cover, a white shirt and a light blue tie enhanced the whole rigout and it looked very smart. They looked splendid and were an honour to their parish.

The uniforms cost £9 each, a total of £162, a fair sum of money in 1959 when a good job paid about £5 a week.

With the assistance of band members John Harford and Joe McGregor, some of those pictured have been identified. Back row, from left to right: Mick Harford, Noel Mooney, Peter Nolan, Larry Lynch, Eugene Tully, Joe McGregor Snr, Eddie Meehan (centre behind drum), Joe McGregor Jnr, Dessie Byrne, Jimmy O'Brien, Charlie Conlon, George Johnston Snr. Front Row: Dessie Manning, Fred Farmer, Patrick Farmer, Sean Fagan and Paddy Buggy.

Blanchardstown Band, 2009, courtesy John Harford, Blanchardstown Brass Band. Exactly fifty years after the band lined out for the 1959 picture, they lined up again in the same place outside the band room and in the same positions. Some of the band members were still there but many had retired or passed away.

The 2009 band are as follows, from left to right: Dermot Byrne, Katcha Manning, John Bates, Johnny Smyth, Zdnek Ondrousek, Joe McGregor, Avril Roche, Morgan Keogh, Mick Harford, John Harford, Eugene Tully, Kevin Harford, Aoife Mulherin, Roy Harford and Paul O'Dwyer.

Incidentally, the band appeared in the feature film *The Yellow Rolls Royce*, made in 1964, starring Rex Harrison, Ingrid Bergman, Shirley McClaine and Omar Sharif.

Mr O'Driscoll was the bandmaster in the 1840s and his direct descendent, Dermot Byrne, is a coronet player in today's band. Mr Brannigan from Chapelizod took over from him. He was followed by Mr Boyne, Mr Ed Smyth, Mr J. Martin (who trained in the Hibernian School) and Mr Larry Lynch, a member of the original Garda Band and the Garda Céilí Band. He was followed by Mr Tommy (Busty) Smyth, Mr Pat O'Brien and Mr Jimmy Lowe, all of the Army School of Music. Mr Billy Byrne, a former conductor of the Garda Band, then took up the baton, followed by Mr Michael Harford, originally from Peck's Lane, and finally Mr Zdenek Ondrousek from the Czech Republic who took over in 2010. He is a graduate of the Conservatory of Music in Pardubice.

Blanchardstown Brass Band Beginners, 1961, courtesy John Harford, Blanchardstown Brass Band. These new recruits to the band are under instruction from Thomas 'Busty' Smith of the Army No. 1 Band. The Blanchardstown Brass Band, founded in 1826, is one of the oldest bands in Ireland.

It was founded by local people involved in a temperance society. Temperance is not like teetotalism – the absolute prohibition of alcohol – but the temperate use of the substance. The consumption of beers and ales were acceptable in moderation whereas strong spirits like whiskey, brandy and gin were deemed unacceptable.

The young lads in the picture are training to be musicians and they are being trained and coached by some of the best musicians in the country. Most of the lads are from the village itself so the band is drawing from a very small well yet the results are fantastic. It probably demonstrates that with education, training and motivation there is music in everyone.

The boys are – back row, from left to right: -?-, Thomas Murphy, ? Brennan, Pat Ford, Mick Power, Frank Norton, Stephen Flynn. Middle row: Brendan Fitzgerald, Robert Norton, Patrick O'Leary, Michael Fitzgerald, -?-, Thomas (Busty) Smith. Front row: Tony Brady, J.J. Maher, ? Brennan, Albert Power, Andrew Valentine, Tony Duffy.

Thanks for the assistance of Joe McGregor, his wife Kathleen and Marie Mulholland with help in identification. Please excuse any incorrect first names as sometimes brothers are very alike.

St Brigid's Pipe Band, 1940s, from *Newswest Year Book*, 1995/96. Photograph supplied originally by Patty Halligan. St Brigid's Pipe Band was formed in 1933 by Paddy Anderson, Denis Farnan, Eddie Hughes and George O'Driscoll.

The founders engaged Mr William Andrews, a native of Scotland, to educate the band in the art of piping. Within a year the band had given their first public performance. By 1936 they were fully fitted out in kilted uniforms. The caps and tunics were made locally by Joseph Thewles, a tailor based in Clonsilla who was a veteran of the War of Independence. The band went further afield for their kilts and where better than Scotland. The band folded in 1946, mainly due to lack of money.

Pictured, from left to right, back row are: Paddy Smith, Ned Hughes, John Malone, John Nulty, Paddy Downey, Sonny Armstrong and John Smith. Front row: Jonnie Stewart, E. O'Neill, Dinny Farnan, Pat Anderson, Nick Anderson and Phil Donegan.

The Old Convent Blanchardstown, photograph by author. This convent was first known as St Brigid's Seminary. Little is known about the seminary until Mother Francis de Sales transferred from the Carmelite Convent in Firhouse to this building opposite the church in Blanchardstown in 1828. The convent catered for the education of girls in the Blanchardstown area up until 1858, when the nuns relocated to Drumcondra.

In 1859 Fr Leman opened the first Holy Ghost Seminary in this building but it did not remain long, moving out to Blackrock, where a fine college was established that is still there today.

Fr Leman introduced the Sisters of St Joseph of Cluny to Dr Cullen, Archbishop of Dublin, and he supported their effort to establish a convent in the building vacated by the Holy Ghost Fathers. Sr Calixte Pichet was the Mother Superior but, being French, did not have full command of the English language and had to send for an English-speaking nun from the mother house in France.

The nuns did not find the convent suitable for use as a boarding school, which was their mission. They spotted an opportunity of buying a large house in its own grounds at Mount Sackville and moved there in 1864.

Since then the building has been used for carpet making, the manufacture of fitted kitchens, offices and nowadays is a Thai restaurant, serving the best of oriental food.

The 12th Lock Royal Canal, Blanchardstown with Granard Bridge in the distance, photograph by author. The Royal Canal is an attractive feature in the area. Built to provide an effective means of transporting bulky goods over long distances, construction commenced in 1790 and it was not completed until 1817. It was less than thirty years in business when the age of steam arrived and left it more or less redundant.

It was suggested at the time that the canal should be drained and the railway run along the dried-out bed. Parliament would not allow this to happen so we have a beautiful linear park stretching all the way from the Liffey to the Shannon.

The Granard Bridge in the distance was named after the Earl of Granard, one of the directors of the canal company.

St Brigid's GAA Club first team, 1932, courtesy Patsy Kelly. St Brigid's GAA Club was founded in 1932 by Johnnie Stewart, Liam Stewart, Pat Anderson, Billy McEntee, Archie McEntee, Paddy Keane, Paddy Smith, Jeremy O'Neill, Billy Monaghan and Jim Mansfield.

In 1935 Tom Russell, the principal of Blanchardstown National School, joined St Brigid's and with his experience, motivation and love for Gaelic games became a great force in the development of the club.

The club purchased the sports field of the Morgan and Mercer's School when it closed down and opened the newly redeveloped grounds in 1979.

Since then other GAA clubs have been formed in the area with the growth of interest in Gaelic football, hurling, handball and camogie. However, Brigid's was the first and Brigid's led the way.

Pictured, from left to right, back row: Baden Powell jnr, unknown, Paddy Smith, S. Kennedy, Pat Anderson, -?-, T. Keogh, J. 'the rep' Sheridan, -?-, Bobby Norton and Jim Smith. Middle row: P. O'Neill, J. Mooney, Bartle O'Neill, M. Halpin and Baden Powell snr. Front row: Johnny Stewart, P. Norton, A. Byrne, Paddy Kelly (captain), A. McEntee and W. Monaghan.

I want to thank two of St Brigid's stalwarts, Jim Fay and Patsy Kelly, for help with identification.

Parslickstown House, once home to the Carr family, photographer unknown. Mulhuddart was once a small village about a mile and a half from Blanchardstown with 120 people living in the village and surrounding farmlands according to *Porters Guide and Directory* from the year 1912.

Some historians believe that Brian Boru rested at Mulhuddart prior to continuing on to his contest with the Viking hordes and their Irish allies at Clontarf.

Mulhuddart is now a thriving suburb of several thousand people. Many of the housing estates take their names from the demesnes, farms and townlands that were often named from previous owners. For instance Huntstown takes its name from the Hunt or de la Hunte family, Tyrellstown from the Tyrell family, barons of Castleknock, Buzzardstown, actually Bossardstown, from the Bossard family and Deanstown from the Dean family.

However, when we come to the name Mulhuddart there is much debate about its origin. According to John O'Donovan's Ordnance Survey Letters of 1833 he has it as Mala, the Brow of a Hill, Hudddart or Hittert. He also speculates that it may be *Mullach Tige Odharnait*, Hill of the House of Odarnat (a Virgin). There was a St Odarnat, whose feast day is 13 November. Other than that, we know nothing of her and if the famous scholar John O'Donovan says she was a virgin who is going to contradict him? The Revd Myles Ronan, who wrote extensively about the Dublin diocese in the mid-twentieth century, favours *Mullach Chuidbert*, Cuthbert's Hill, after the Northumbrian saint of that name who was said to be the son of an Irish king. Another source gives it as *Maolaedard*, 'the high place of the sun's fire'. If you were standing on the hill on a summer's evening, watching the setting sun in the west, you could see how it would have been so named.

The Carr family lived in Parslickstown House and some sources say that the first Carr to arrive in the area was a survivor of the Battle of Tara Hill, fought on 26 May 1798. The insurgents outnumbered the government forces but had few firearms, no artillery, no cavalry and no training or experience. Over 400 were killed against total government losses of 30 men. It's said that one of the insurgents, a youth named Carr from County Wexford, made his way from the battlefield to Mulhuddart and was looked after there and settled in the community.

There is an incredible yarn that years later Frank Carr, a son of this man, witnessed a public execution in England. The condemned man was given the chance of saying some last words and said in a strong voice, 'Is there any among you from Mulhudddart?' Mr Carr answered 'yes' and he was directed by the condemned man to go to Blair's Wall (in some versions of the story it is Blair's Well) where he would find a crock of gold. He discovered the gold and with it purchased Parlickstown's 164 acres in or about 1840.

Curiously, during the War of Independence local children found a cache of gold sovereigns near the same spot. It is reported that the local unit of the IRA swept into the village and took the lot to buy munitions.

New Holland Mills in Strawberry Beds was at one time an iron factory owned by a Mr Blair and it was raided by rebel forces prior to the Battle of Tara. Whether or not this has any connection to the treasure horde I don't know.

Whatever about the Battle of Tara and the crock of gold, Frank Carr did have great foresight. When the potato crop first failed in 1844 Carr got hold of all the turnip seed he could lay his hands on and sowed a massive amount of this seed on his lands. Carr's brainwave did much to lessen the impact of the famine in this area.

Local men tidying up Lady's Well, Mulhuddart, courtesy Fingal County Council. This famous well has been a site of pilgrimage for centuries. The well was originally dedicated to St Cuthbert of Melrose Abbey and Lindisfarne. In the early thirteenth century it was rededicated to the Virgin Mary.

The feast days of the Blessed Virgin attracted many pilgrims to the well on patron day and whenever crowds gather business follows. In medieval times 25 March, the Feast of the Annunciation, was the first day of the year and was known as Lady's Day and this continued up until 1752. This day attracted large crowds to the well as did 15 August, the Feast of the Assumption, and 8 December, the Feast of the Immaculate Conception. The biggest gathering was on 8 September, the Blessed Virgin's birthday, and people travelled from far and wide.

Booths were set up around the shrine selling religious pictures and trinkets, food and other goods and services. The main problem was the many booths that sold a liquid that was as far from holy water as one could imagine. Poteen and rough gin and other types of fire water were for sale and the result was often fist fighting, drunkenness, gambling and other unseemly activity. Incidentally there were reputed to be nine cures in the well water and – you couldn't make this up – one cure was for sore heads!

The Church and the authorities eventually decided to call a halt. When Fr Mathew's temperance movement commenced in 1838, Fr Dungan introduced novenas in St Brigid's church to coincide with patron day and the Mulhuddart festival ceased.

The men decorating the well in the picture are demonstrating the true spirit of what the well means. They are from, left to right: Pat 'Boley' Byrne, Ned Hughes and Richie Clarke.

The Farnan family outside their home on Segrave's farm near Cloghran, in the early 1930s, courtesy Marie Cummins. The Farnan family were very active in the War of Independence. Not only did their young men risk their lives in the fight for Irish freedom but they also allowed their lands and outhouses to be used for training and for the storing of war material. One of them, Paddy, was killed in the Battle of the Four Courts.

Pictured kneeling at the front is Jimmy Farnan Snr with a little boy, Jimmy Farnan Jnr, and, from left to right: baby May Farnan (later Farmer), Mary Farnan, Mickey Farnan, May Anderson (who later married Nicky), James Farnan (the grandfather), Dinny Farnan, Mary Farnan (the grandmother *née* Byrne) and Nellie Farnan (later Hogan).

This area of Cloghran has a townland called Godamendy and there is a quarry close by known as the Mare and Foal. There is a legend concerning a priest saying Mass at a mass rock there in Penal times. There is a ruined chapel there where it would have been safe to have a Mass said without endangering the priest.

At the most solemn part of the Mass one of the lookouts approached the priest to tell him that a thief was attempting to steal his mare and her foal, tethered in the nearby quarry. The priest raised his eyes towards the heavens and intoned in a loud voice, 'May God amend ye!' and at that the mare and foal were rooted to the spot. The marks of their hooves in the stone of the quarry could be seen until recent times.

A cycle race at Jones' Road Sports Ground (now Croke Park), courtesy Fingal County Council. Herbie Breedon, Frank Baird and Bertie Donnelly appear in this picture dating back to the late 1920s. This trio dominated the sport, then in its infancy in Ireland. Bertie Donnelly and later his son Sean owned the Shanty Pub in Mulhuddart Village.

Bertie represented Ireland in the 1928 Olympics in Amsterdam and did well in the cycling events but did not win a medal. In 1933 he partnered Herbie Breedon from St Patrick's Park Blanchardstown in the Irish Tandem Championships and they won the 25-mile title. Both were members of the Harp Cycling Club. Coincidentally both of them died within hours of each other on the same day in November 1977 and are buried a couple of yards apart in Mulhuddart Cemetery.

4

CABRA, PELLETSTOWN & CARDIFF'S BRIDGE

Cabra, Pelletstown and Cardiff's Bridge are all on the border of Castleknock Barony where it meets the Barony of Nethercross along the Tolka River near Finglas and the old Coolock Barony, later known as the Barony of Dublin city at the manor of Grangegorman.

Cabra was divided into Much Cabragh and Little Cabragh and derives its name from the Irish word for rough land or poor land.

I grew up in the area and found the soil in Cabra to be very fertile and easily worked. The cottage gardens at Convent View, where I lived, were extensively cultivated and the families who lived there since 1909, when the cottages were built, grew flowers for the Dublin market. They continued to grow the flowers there until Dublin Corporation acquired the gardens by compulsory purchase order in 1970.

Up till the late 1600s, much of Cabragh was covered by a large wood known as Salcock's Wood. The Ballyboggan area where the headwaters of the Bradogue River and other smaller streams rise was very swampy. There were several large quarries in that area where in some places stones may have been close to the surface. The Tolka valley was prone to flooding and marshlands existed on both sides of the river.

The River Tolka at Cardiff's Bridge attracted anglers from far and wide and it was not unknown for an angler to pull twenty or more trout from that spot in an evening. I remember as a young fellow paddling around in the waters underneath the bridge, turning over the stones that lay on the riverbed in pursuit of a grub, a little creature that lived beneath the stones that anglers called 'corbait'. This grub was irresistible to trout and an old jam jar of these little creatures could be exchanged in return for a few pennies from the anglers.

Cardiff's Bridge is named from the Kerdiff family whose ancestors arrived with the Normans. They had a castle, Kerdiff's Castle, in nearby Finglas.

In nearby Scribblestown lived Lady Eva Forbes, sister of Lord Granard. Her gleaming black 1927 14.9 Ford limousine was much admired by local people as it whisked her down to Sunday Mass in St Peter's church, Phibsborough.

On the road leading to Cabra from Cardiff's Bridge a road turned off to the left towards Finglas Bridge. This road was called Ballyboggan Road but had another name: The King's Lane. It takes its name from the ruin of a very old manor house belonging to the Segrave family located where Ballyboggan Road meets Broombridge Road. This ruin, once used as a tannery and demolished since 1970, was known locally as King James's Castle from a local legend that King James II stayed there on the night of his defeat at the Battle of the Boyne. Most authorities say that he spent that night in Dublin Castle. King William's army did stay in Finglas after that battle and locals point to an area called King William's Ramparts as the site of the camp.

The local story goes that King James II, seeing the rout of his army at the Boyne, swung his horse's head around towards Dublin and with a kick of his spurs propelled his steed in that direction with the utmost alacrity. While careering down King's Lane he met with Lady Ormonde, the wife of his Commander in Chief, who sweetly enquired how the day had gone. 'Your cowardly Irish have ran away – fled the field – raced away from the enemy,' an ashen-faced King James blustered, all the while looking fearfully around to his rear. 'Indeed, your Majesty,' responded Lady Ormonde, 'and I see that it is you that has won the race', and turning around on her heel she left him speechless, sitting astride his horse on that narrow country lane.

On the approach to Cabra from Cardiff's Bridge is St Mary's Dominican Convent. The nuns moved there in 1819 from Clontarf, where they stayed for a short time, having vacated their house in Channell Row. Prior to that the nuns had their convent in Galway.

The Penal Laws came into force when the nuns were in Galway and they had to keep a low profile. They moved to Channell Row from there and during their time there the Penal Laws were renewed with much vigour in 1743. A reward of £150 was offered for information leading to the arrest of a bishop and £50 reward for a priest. In 1744 a Fr Nicholas English was seized from the altar of St Paul's church, Dublin, while saying Mass and cast into prison. That same year two other priests were captured in Channell Row

Convent and imprisoned. However, in 1745 the Penal laws were relaxed as the Jacobite Rising led by Bonnie Prince Charlie had broken out in Scotland and the authorities wanted to mollify the Irish for fear the rising would spread to Ireland. By the time the nuns took up residence in Cabra they were free to carry out their mission without hindrance.

Fr Thomas McNamara, a very famous Vincentian, and Monsignor Yore, suggested to the Dominican nuns that they might consider opening a school for the education of girls with impaired hearing. At this stage the Dominican nuns had founded a girls school and a boys school in Cabra and both schools were up and running. While Fathers McNamara and Yore were discussing the merits of the school for the deaf with the Dominican nuns they were also in negotiations with the Irish Christian Brothers, exploring the possibilities of a school for boys with impaired hearing.

The Dominican Convent's property of Little Cabra was originally built by the Segrave family in 1597. The family predate the Norman invasion and were a key family in the area for many years. Their name springs from the Teutonic language and translates as Sea Lord. They were of Scandinavian origin, possibly arriving at the time of Viking raids. At the Battle of Clontibret Capt. James Segrave fought Hugh O'Neill, the Irish chieftain, in single combat. O'Neill was overpowered by Segrave's superior strength but before Segrave delivered the *coup de grâce*, O'Neill mortally wounded him with his dagger.

John Toler, 1st Lord Norbury, occupied the Segrave property from the late 1700s up until his death in 1831. Norbury had a fearful reputation and was a keen supporter of capital punishment. At one session of the assizes he sentenced 198 prisoners to death by hanging. For this he became known as the Hanging Judge. He was also a politician. He did much to bring about the Act of Union that dissolved the Irish Parliament. His work for the government was rewarded with a peerage and the post of Lord Chief Justice. He died at the age of 85 in 1831. At his funeral it was reported that the ropes provided to lower his coffin into the grave were found to be too short for purpose. Runners were sent to get longer ropes and a voice from the crowd shouted, 'Get plenty for he never spared it on others'.

It is said that his ghost haunts the area and he has been seen galloping on horseback; others say he takes the shape of a huge mastiff with glaring bloodshot eyes and drags clanking chains along the lanes of Cabra.

The Segraves moved back into Little Cabragh House after Norbury's death. Charles Segrave was the last of the family to reside there. Charles's son Henry was a famed racing driver and at one time held the land speed record and the water speed record.

The last person to live in Little Cabragh House was Phil Callaghan, a nephew of the Byrne family who had it after Charles Segrave. The Reid family of Cabra Farm stayed there for a while following a fire at their Cabra Farm home in 1934. The house was demolished by Dublin Corporation in 1939.

All that remains of this great house is a fine Chippendale that resides in an even finer home – Dublin Castle, where it is used in one of the State apartments.

There is a stream flowing through Cabra called the Bradogue. Its headwaters are near Broombridge and it flows underground through Cabra on a circuitous route. It is the Channell that Channell Row takes its name from and is associated with the name Broadstone where the bus depot is. It flowed into the Liffey at a circular pond in the river called The Pill, near today's fruit market. Another stream coming from the same headwaters flows underground from Broombridge and is associated with a well that was opposite the fine arched entrance to the Dominican convent. It flows along the boundary of Convent View and along the line of the wall of Pope John Paul II Park (the Bogies), where it is culverted. It forms a pond at the rear of where the old handball alley stood and passes under the aptly named Brook Shop. There it passes under the Navan Road along the gardens of Roosevelt Cottages, under Blackhorse Lane near Primrose Cottage, where it is associated with the Poor Man's Well, and into the Phoenix Park, where it fills the small ornamental lake at Áras an Uachtaráin known as the Lord's Lake.

The North and South County Dublin Unions (The Poorhouse) faced each other on Navan Road. When the Poor Law system was disestablished they became St Vincent's – a home for children and adults with special needs – and St Patrick's – a mother and baby home with a Magdalene laundry. St Vincent's has done great work and is still fulfilling its mission. It's managed by the Daughters of Charity of St Vincent de Paul and has been there since 1892. St Patrick's Home, or Pelletstown, as it was known, was founded about the same time and was run by the same order. Between 1940 and 1970, 254 children born there were sent to the United States for adoption. It was knocked down in 1985 and the lands were developed for housing. Current investigations reveal that there was a high mortality rate amongst the children who were born there.

The whole parish of St Mary Help of Christians on the Navan Road and a good portion of the parish of the Most Precious Blood were part of Chapelizod parish up till the 1940s – the 1950s in the case of the former – and prior to that both were part of St Brigid's, Blanchardstown.

Cardiff's Bridge, 1838, drawing by Adam Lacey after a contemporary drawing by B. King. The large house at the top left of the picture was occupied by the Hoey family for years and was previously occupied by a salesmaster in the cattle market named Newman. The Newmans bred Angora rabbits. These rabbits originated in Turkey near the city and region of Ankara. They were prized for the softness, fineness and fluffiness of their wood. The meat of the rabbits was also very palatable.

The building to the right of the picture was an old mill that later became a spade factory. The bridge is no longer used and a new bridge nearby carries the Ratoath Road over the River Tolka.

Next to the Hoeys up the road towards Finglas lived the Maffet family of Springmount, (locals always called them Moffats). The last of the family to live there was Gerald Edward, who died suddenly in 1936. Gerald's father, W.H. Maffat, was a barrister and his brother Oswald was a district inspector in the RIC. Gerald was involved in breeding and training horses and at one time worked in the accounts section of the GPO. The family were cousins of the Harmsworth family in Chapelizod, which included Lord Northcliffe and his brothers, who were prominent in the newspaper and publishing business.

The river was famed for the quality, size and abundance of its trout and anglers flocked from far and wide to fish there. Such was the quantity of trout one character known as Lumpy Brown walked the river (and I mean walked in the river) from here to Drumcondra wearing a long coat with deep pockets. He was able to tickle the trout and put them in his pockets as he went. Unfortunately the quality of the waters deteriorated in the 1960s due to leachate from the city dump at Dunsink beside a tributary of the Tolka and also because of uncontrolled pollution from commercial activities.

The good news is that the Tolka is now a living river once more with trout breeding successfully and salmon have reappeared after an absence of 100 years.

Cardiff's Bridge, *c.* 1936, photographer unknown. Cardiff's Bridge was a small village up until the 1950s. In the picture you can see the old iron mill to the left of the bridge, which became a spade and shovel factory in the mid-1800s. It was a man named James Tyrrell who transformed the mill, possibly about 1860. It is believed that he encouraged some of the workers to migrate from Newry, where there was experience in the manufacture of these tools.

The original mill was built by the Dillons of Keppock (Cappagh) who sold it to the Kerdiffs in 1577. The mill and the bridge were named after the Kerdiff family and over the years the name was corrupted into Cardiff. The millrace drew its water from the Tolka 800m upstream, near the sharp bend in the road at Anderson's Pelletstown House gate lodge. For a while Pelletstown House was home to John French, a young officer who later became a field marshal in the First World War and later Viceroy of Ireland.

The ruins of a very old castle were here until about sixty years ago. It may have been a tower house castle built by the Kerdiff family to protect the millrace. The family probably lived here before building Kerdiff's Castle close to Finglas village. Alas this castle is long gone too. At some stage, probably mid-1800s, the mill changed over to steam. Its tall redbrick chimney was visible for miles around.

The cottage on the far side of the river is all that was left of the buildings that included the public house known as the Jolly Toper. Joseph O'Keeffe was the licensee for years and although the pub was miles from the sea it was a favourite watering hole for mariners. Outside the pub hung a sign depicting a couple of drinkers (topers) knocking back pints with beaming smiles on their faces. It had a pretty little green dotted with flowers with outdoor seating provided. On Saturday afternoons patrons of the sport of wrestling, then a popular sport in north County Dublin, would come in droves to enjoy the bouts. There was also a skittles alley out the back of the pub and musicians came along in the evenings to add to the various attractions.

The Finnegan family took over the licence from the O'Keeffes in the 1920s but later on they discontinued the pub business. Rose 'Cosy' Finnegan continued to operate a small grocery shop until the late 1950s.

Serious flooding in December 1954, when the Tolka burst its banks, persuaded the people living in the cottages at the bridge to relocate and by the late 1960s most of the villagers had left also. The road was diverted and a new bridge and a wider road carries traffic from Cabra to Ratoath or into Finglas. The old Cardiff's Bridge is still there, now within the Tolka Valley Park.

The Broken Arch Swimming Pool, also known as Cabra Baths, *c.* 1950s, courtesy Martin Coffey. The outdoor pool on Ballyboggan Road took its name from the remains of a single-arch bridge that stood at the spot where the pool was located and was built by Dublin Corporation in 1944, mainly through the offices of Alderman Martin O'Sullivan of the Labour Party. The pool was very popular with the boys from Cabra and Finglas.

On the day of the official opening the clergyman who was given the honour of blessing the pool recoiled in horror when he saw the boys and girls splashing around. He immediately ordered the girls out – mixed bathing, even for kids, was a no-no in 1940s Ireland. The clergyman's rule held until the pool closed down in 1971. The boys swam in the chlorinated waters of the pool drawn from the River Tolka while the girls splashed around in the muddy waters of the Tolka. It must be said that most of the boys when they hit 14 years of age forsook the chlorinated waters of the pool for the muddier but more alluring waters where the girls swam.

Another swimming spot further down the road, near the ruins of King James Castle (in reality Savages Tannery), was very popular for generations. It was at a very deep slate quarry adjoining the river and was known as the Silver Spoon. It was an idyllic beauty spot and a Finglas man called Brendan Devereux wrote a beautiful song called 'The Silver Spoon' about this delightful place. It is on his *Copper Alley* album and is available on YouTube. Dublin Corporation, in their corporate wisdom, selected this beautiful spot as the site for a city dump in the 1950s. In the early 1970s they covered the refuse and seeded it with grass and landscaped it. To those who do not know what lies beneath it looks very pleasant.

Chapel of Dominican convent, Cabra, Lawrence Collection, courtesy National Library of Ireland. The chapel of the Dominican convent in Cabra was built between 1851 and 1852 and is the work of John Bourke, an architect who designed many church-related projects at that time. He was associated with the building of the Mater Hospital 1855 and the church of the Nativity Chapelizod 1844/49.

The foundation stone of the new chapel was laid on 18 August 1851 and dedicated by the Most Revd Dr Paul Cullen, Archbishop of Dublin on 28 December 1852. The chapel was dedicated to Jesus, Mary and Joseph.

A relic of St Oliver Plunkett (part of his arm bone) was presented to the convent in 1872 by Dr Moran Archbishop of Ossory.

The chapel was completely renovated in 1904/05 under the architectural supervision of George Coppinger Ashlin of Ashlin & Coleman and it was extended at the front and a new façade was added.

The chapel has a painting of the crucifixion attributed to Anthony Van Dyck. The chapel is beautiful and includes a particularly fine set of the Stations of the Cross from Bruges in Belgium. There is also a mosaic depicting various Dominican saints, the work of Oppenheimer. It's said to be one of their finest mosaics.

Oratory of Expiation, Dominican convent, Cabra, courtesy Olivia Leonard, 'The Past and Present Blanchardstown and Surrounding Areas', Online History Group. On 31 July 1829, while the nuns of St Mary's Dominican Convent were attending their annual retreat, local people noticed suspicious-looking characters loitering in the vicinity of the convent.

That night the chapel (not the present one as it was not built until 1852) was broken into and sacred vessels – silver candlesticks, a silver monstrance and a ciborium containing consecrated hosts were stolen. Following the theft the thieves became hopelessly lost in the convent grounds. One of them, a woman who was later arrested, made a confession. She described how they were unable to escape the grounds and it seemed some power was preventing their escape. They decided to empty the ciborium containing the hosts on the ground near a tree and a while later they were able to make their escape.

The nuns did not discover the theft until the following morning and started to search the grounds. They discovered the hosts alongside the Lime Walk and retrieved them and also recovered one of the sacred vessels. They pledged to build an oratory on the spot where they retrieved the consecrated hosts. They eventually built the Oratory of Expiation in 1884 at that same spot on the Lime Walk. It was refurbished in recent years and it is a very beautiful small chapel.

Arched gateway of St Mary's Dominican convent, early 1900s, from an old photograph in the author's possession. The beautiful arched gate of St Mary's and the convent chapel with its twin onion-shaped domes is a well-known landmark in north County Dublin. The beautiful arched entrance gate was erected in 1867. The design is unattributed but I believe it may be the work of John Bourke.

Many local people in times gone by worked as agricultural workers on the farm and did maintenance work in the convent and its grounds. Today teachers are employed, as are specialist workers with experience in training and education of the deaf, and there are also facilities for the blind and deaf on site.

The nuns were cloistered until the mid-1960s and if they had to travel outside it was in a car with drawn curtains and blinds driven by their chauffeur Mr Matthew Reid, a veteran of the First World War and a real gentleman.

The Dominican convent accommodated many Church dignitaries during the Eucharistic Congress of 1932. During the visit of Pope John Paul II to Ireland in 1979 he stayed in the Papal Nuncio's residence in the convent grounds and visited St Mary's School for Deaf Girls where he met representatives from the other churches in the Dominican convent.

During the visit Cabra and the surrounding area was covered with flags and buntings. When the decorations were all removed and all the dignitaries had departed a witty Cabra woman with a great turn of phrase said she was suffering from post-Papal depression!

Little Cabragh House, photographer unknown. This was a big house, despite its name, and was built by the Segrave family around 1597. It was built of stone, had tiled roofs and was surrounded by gardens and orchards. It was set in a beautiful parkland dotted with tall ornamental trees. It boasted a brewery, dairy, malt-house, stables, barns, a byre, a coach house and a chapel – along with a secret priest's chamber, a false chimney and hidden passages. It was located near the present-day Canon Burke Flats.

The Segraves were Recusants, i.e. Roman Catholics who did not recognise royal authority in religious matters, and protected priests and provided a venue for Mass during Penal times. The Segraves were otherwise loyal supporters of the Crown and as such held on to their possessions and were not interfered with in the practice of their religion.

After John Segrave died the property fell into the possession of Denis Daly (Lord Dunstable's father) for a short while. Lord Norbury then leased it from the late 1700s until his death in 1831. Lord Norbury had a bad reputation and was feared and hated. He was said to be a bigot and the son of a bigot. He detested the Irish peasantry and their religion and was fond of pronouncing the death sentence. Stories relating to his ghost appearing at various places around his old home are eagerly recounted. He appears as a headless horseman but the fact that he retained his head up till his death takes a little from the stories.

The Segraves moved back after Norbury's death but their stays were intermittent. Charles Segrave was the last of the family to live there and left in 1912; he was followed by Mary Donnelly, Peter Heany, the Byrne family, the Reid family and Phil Callaghan, who all lived in the house before it was briefly used as a storehouse for the Irish Glass Bottle Co. It was demolished in 1939.

John Toler, 1st Earl of Norbury, Chief Justice of the Irish Common Pleas (1745-1831), painting attributed to James John Russell, courtesy The Honourable Society of King's Inns.

Lord Norbury was born at Beechwood Nenagh, County Tipperary, and was the son of Cromwellian settlers. Following his graduation from university he was called to the Irish Bar in 1770. He was elected as MP for Tralee and later MP for Philipstown (now Daingean) and then for Gorey – all seats in the Irish Parliament. He supported the Act of Union and was made Chief Justice of the Common Pleas and raised to the peerage as a reward.

His knowledge of law was poor and his decisions and judgement were often biased. He had a weird sense of humour, joking and laughing while handing down death sentences. While passing a death sentence on a child pickpocket he dryly remarked, 'You grasped for time but you've now caught eternity'.

Norbury was short in stature and had a jovial demeanour, with tiny grey twinkling eyes and a peculiar habit of puffing out his cheeks, which earned him the nickname 'Puffendor'.

He was an accomplished duellist and was fearless, even challenging the Lord Lieutenant to a duel at eighty years of age. Lord Norbury died in 1831 at his town house 3 Denmark Street.

Major Henry Segrave (1896-1930), photographer unknown. Henry O'Neill de Hane Segrave was born in Baltimore, Maryland, USA, in 1896. He was the son of Charles Segrave, the last of the Segrave dynasty to live in Little Cabragh House.

He served in the Royal Flying Corps in the First World War and during that time he became interested in motor racing. He went on to win the French Grand Prix in 1923, followed by the San Sebastian Grand Prix in Spain in 1924. He was the first motor racer to wear a crash helmet and promoted its use to such an extent that it was incorrectly believed that he invented it.

He achieved the top land speed record at 152.33mph (245.15km/h) in 1926, driving a 4-litre Sunbeam Tiger. He became the first driver to exceed 200mph in 1927, in a Sunbeam fitted with an aeronautical engine said to be 1,000hp. In 1929 he set a third record of 231.44mph.

He also became interested in racing motorboats and won the International Championship in Florida in 1928. He was knighted in 1929 for his contribution to motor sports.

On Friday, 13 June 1930 he was fatally injured while bettering his own world record driving *Miss England II* on Lake Windermere, achieving a speed of 85.8 knots (98.76mph). In a second run he crashed after striking a submerged log. Segrave was taken from the water but a broken rib had pierced his lung and he lived only long enough to learn he had achieved the world record. His wife Doris was at the scene and he passed away in her arms. His ashes were scattered from an aircraft over the playing fields of Eton, his old Alma Mater, by his father.

Frederick William Reid (on the left) of Cabra Farm at Easter Parade in St Stephen's Green, c. 1940, courtesy Elizabeth Reid. Frederick Reid was a market gardener who employed many local people at Cabra Farm, where vegetable crops were grown for the Dublin market. Cabra Farm was centred on a house of the same name located where the crossroads intersection of Navan Road and Nephin Road is today.

Frederick Reid is pictured here in the uniform of the Local Security Force in 1940. At the outset of the Emergency the LSF was a reserve force for the military. It was then divided into the Local Defence Force, the Army Reserve Force and the Local Security Force, later called Taca, that was Garda Reserve Force.

There was a serious risk of an invasion from either Axis Forces or Allied Forces. Our defence forces conducted military manoeuvres and practised war games along a northern line, centred on the River Boyne and in the south along the river Blackwater. These shows of military strength gave the necessary message that we were not a pushover and any potential invasion would meet with resistance.

Flooding at Blackhorse Lane (now Avenue), late 1930s, picture from the *Evening Mail*, courtesy Elizabeth Reid. There are many small rivers in Cabra – some are associated with the Bradogue. The Phoenix Park has several streams associated with it. The name Phoenix is a corruption of the Irish *Fionn Uisce*, meaning fair water or bright water. In the Down Survey Ashtown's bounds are 'on the east with Little Cabragh, South with Ffenix (*Fionn Uisce*), on the west Castleknock, on the North the Toulchy (Tolka) water'.

Most sources suggest the *Fionn Uisce* was a well and place it variously near the Magazine Fort or the zoo grounds or inside the gate of Áras an Uachtaráin or confuse it with the Poor Man's Well at Cabra Gate. The Down Survey describes it as a boundary, indicating it must have length. The boundary so described is now an underground stream that rises in the region of Deerpark Estate at Castleknock Gate and continues on to parallel the Chesterfield Road through Phoenix Park. The stream surfaces at Mountjoy corner as the Machine Pond, as a pond in Áras an Uachtaráin, as a small lake in the zoo and finally as a pond in the People's Gardens before entering the Liffey near the railway tunnel.

These underground rivers come up to say hello at times of heavy rains and we are all familiar with floods near the Castleknock Gate in Phoenix Park and the junction of Navan Road and Blackhorse Lane and lots of other places in the locality.

The man drawing the horse and cart in the picture is Bob Fagan of Roosevelt Cottages. The first boy boarding the cart is Tom Reid and he is followed by Tony McCrae.

Primrose Cottage, Blackhorse Avenue. Artist Eugene Kennedy executed the painting in 2013, based on memory and old photographs, specifically for this book. This cottage was one of only two thatched cottages remaining within the Dublin City boundary. The thatch was replaced with a mansard roof in the late 1970s.

Primrose Cottage was owned by the Tuite family who grew fruit, flowers and vegetables on the property. The Lawlor family, who later owned the cottage, were direct descendants of the Tuites. The cottage and its delightful garden were much commented on by visitors to the area. In spring the scent of the apple blossoms from the orchard filled the air and in the autumn the branches of the trees were laden with rosy red apples. Many youngsters from the area, in an effort to alleviate the strain from the struggling branches, selflessly negotiated the high hedge and wire barrier with their only reward a succulent apple or two or maybe more. I plead guilty.

The walls of Primrose Cottage are immensely thick and are slanted to throw off water. The cottage would appear to be very old and could date back to mid-1600s or earlier.

5

CASTLEKNOCK VILLAGE, CASTLEKNOCK COLLEGE & KNOCKMAROON

Castleknock, particularly the surroundings of the castle and St Brigid's church, seem to be the earliest areas of settlement in the barony. The area, now within the confines of Castleknock College, including the twin mounds, has a history going back to a time when it is difficult to separate history from myth.

The peasantry who inhabited Castleknock at the time of the Norman Conquest were probably ill-treated enough by whichever Irish chieftain they had been ruled by so their lives may not have changed significantly with the arrival of the Anglo-Normans. They would have continued to have been treated little better than the livestock in the field. In fact, the livestock were better fed as they were being fattened for the market. The peasants' lives meant nothing and they could be executed for the paltriest of crimes.

However, what the Anglo-Normans did bring was organisation and government. They also engaged in land improvement, drainage and crop rotation and fertilised the land. They changed the main type of agriculture from pasture to tillage. The society that exists today evolved from this original feudal system but it took many years of turmoil and revolution and still there are haves and have-nots.

Castleknock developed slowly and the Castleknock of the late 1800s and early 1900s would have been not unfamiliar to people who lived there at the time of the Norman Conquest.

Castleknock Castle 1791, painting by Eugene Kennedy from a copy of Cocking's drawing in *Grose's Antiquities*. In May 1169, the first group of Norman invaders landed at Bannow Bay and captured Wexford. Another force, which landed at the cove of Baginbun, re-enforced them. Richard de Clare, known as 'Strongbow', led the rest of the army to capture Waterford.

They had arrived at the invitation of Dermot McMurrough, king of Leinster, who had been embroiled in a dispute with the High King Rory O'Connor who was also King of Connaught. By the summer of 1171 Dublin had been captured by the Normans and King Rory O'Connor assembled a large force of Irish warriors and laid siege to it. A fleet of thirty ships of King Rory's Norse allies lay at anchor at Dublin Bay to prevent relief by sea. The siege left the Normans in Dublin city in great difficulty and they sought terms of surrender.

Maurice de Prendergast accompanied Bishop Laurence O'Toole, who was acting as mediator, to Rory's encampment at Castleknock. An army laying siege to a city can often become lax and undisciplined due to inactivity. De Prendergast was a shrewd commander and noted that the Irish army were not a fighting force to be reckoned with and that their encampment was not adequately guarded. He reported this back to Strongbow and Strongbow commanded Miles de Cogan to lead a party of knights to attack the Castleknock encampment under cover of darkness. De Cogan split his forces, sending one party of knights directly from Stoneybatter to Castleknock for a frontal attack while the remainder of the force went around by Finglas to attack from the rear.

The Normans struck at dawn, taking the Irish completely by surprise; Rory himself, who was taking a bath in the Liffey near Glenmaroon at that time, had to flee in a state of royal nudity.

Later that year King Henry II arrived in Dublin and accepted Strongbow as King of Leinster. However, he brought with him Hugh de Lacy and granted him the old fifth province of Meath to act as a counterbalance to Strongbow. De Lacy granted the 12,000 acres of Castleknock to his man Hugh Tyrrell. Copies of the charters of Hugh de Lacy and King Henry II granting Castleknock to Tyrrell were discovered in the London Public Records Office in 1933 by Eric St John Brooks. These copies of the originals date back to 1293 and are entirely in Latin – the language for most legal documents of that time.

The grant is translated thus:

Henry, by the grace of God, King of England, Lord of Ireland, Duke of Aquitane and Normandy and Count of Anjou to the Archbishops, Bishops, Ministers and all Earls, Barons, Justices, Sheriffs, Ministers and all his faithful French, English and Irish, greeting. Know that I have conceded, given, and by present Charter confirmed to Hugh Tirel, the man of Hugh de Lacy, Thwothyn and Thwothrom.

The witnesses to the documents are mostly high-ranking Norman noblemen and clergy and include one Stephen Pilat, who gave his name to the nearby townland of Pelletstown. Another, Adam de Feipo, gave his name to Phibsborough.

The names Thwothyn and Thwothrom for Castleknock seem to be an attempt to represent the Irish word *tuath* (territory). Thwothrom may be derived from the Irish '*tuath droma*', meaning the area of the ridge or hill, probably the hill of Castleknock.

The barony takes its name from Tyrrell's Castle, built about 1190 on the site of what was originally a Viking fort that in turn was built on an Irish dún. The 'knock' part of the name relates to a lady named Cnucha. It has nothing to do with the Irish *cnoc*, meaning a hill. Cnuacha was the wife of Genann or Genam, who was said to have ruled Ireland as a high king jointly with his brother Gann. They were the sons of Dela who was a Fir Bolg or Milesian chieftain who arrived in Ireland about 1000 BC. This information comes from a book called *The Book of Invasions*, a compilation of old stories, poems, legends and folklore written in the eleventh century. Many scholars consider it to be completely mythological; however, the legends indicated that we are descended from people who originated in northern Spain and recently a study of Irish DNA has confirmed it.

Cnucha, some sources say, was the foster mother of Conn of the Hundred Battles. She is said to be buried in the centre of the mound at Castleknock. Cumhall, the father of Fionn Mac Cumhaill, who was slain by Goll MacMorna at the Battle of Cnucha, was also buried in the mound.

The hill of Castleknock is the easternmost point of the Esker Riada, a series of ridges that run through counties Galway, Roscommon, Offaly, Westmeath, Kildare and Dublin. It was used as a natural route connecting the west coast of Ireland with the east coast and was known as *An tSlí Mor*. The Esker Riada was formed from the meltwaters of the glaciers that covered most of the country during the ice age. The hill that the castle was built on and the hill known as Windmill Hill or Tower Hill are geological features.

Castleknock castle in the mid-eighteenth century, painting by Gabriel Beranger, courtesy National Library of Ireland. The castle at this stage was in ruins as a result of the various sieges and battles.

Gabriel Beranger came here from Antwerp. His family were originally Huguenot refugees from France. I think the quality and beauty of his paintings are of great value to the cultural history of Castleknock.

The castle built by Hugh Tyrrell was originally a motte-and-bailey castle but was eventually reconstructed with high walls and a multi-angular design.

Following the arrival of Hugh Tyrrell and his followers Castleknock changed from being a small settlement in a clearing between the Great Scaldwood and the vast woods that covered what is today's Phoenix Park to a thriving village surrounded by well-tilled fields.

Castleknock watchtower and castle at a distance by Gabriel Beranger, courtesy National Library of Ireland. When we ramble around the ivy-covered remains of these old castles and abbeys we might remember the peasants who toiled in the fields from first light to after sunset. It was their labours that created the landscape we see before us. They uprooted the trees, they tilled and drained the land and sowed the crops.

Eight barons of Castleknock occupied the castle for 200 years. Hugh, the first baron, was succeeded by Richard, the second baron, who was succeeded by Hugh, the third baron, and then Richard, the fourth baron. Hugh, the fifth baron, took over in 1295 and was followed by the sixth baron in 1299. His son, Hugh, inherited the title of seventh baron in 1364 although still a minor. Hugh's son Robert died in 1370, along with his wife Scholastica, from the Black Plague which was sweeping Europe at the time. This ended the Tyrrell dynasty. The castle and lands passed to Robert's two sisters Joan and Matilda. Joan's second husband, William Boltham, held the castle until 1408. When he died, his stepson, Thomas Serjeant, son of Joan's first husband, got possession of it.

The estate remained in the family until Chief Justice Sir Nicholas Barnwell secured it through marriage. It then passed to Roland Eustace, Baron of Portlester, and then to the Burnell family. The Burnell interest arose through John Burnell, the second husband of Matilda Tyrrell. Henry Burnell, John's son, was a brilliant lawyer who represented the Irish cause at the royal court in London. He argued strongly for the repeal of Poynings' Law, which subjected the Irish to all English laws. He also petitioned for toleration of the Roman Catholic faith in Ireland.

In 1641 the castle was secured for the Irish forces under Owen Roe O'Neill. It was recaptured by General Monck who diverted his march to Athlone to attack the castle. In 1647 Owen Roe retook the castle.

In the Down Survey Christopher Barnwell is shown as proprietor of the castle and lands of 232 acres. However, the property was in mortgage to William Warren of Corduff. The Warren family farmed the lands and eventually sold them in the early 1800s.

Such was the devastation caused in the barony during the mid-1600s by the various wars the land became untamed and the Great Scaldwood of Blanchardstown, once succumbed to the plough, returned to dense forest. Wolves, which were always present in the forest, increased in number and the authorities had to initiate a massive wolf-cull in 1652. This is the last record that we have of wolves in this area. Within a couple of decades the wolf became extinct in Ireland, the last wolf being killed on the slopes of Mount Leinster, County Carlow, in 1786.

Castleknock church, by Gabriel Beranger, courtesy National Library of Ireland. The church depicted in Gabriel Beranger's painting was built in 1609. It replaced the old abbey of St Brigid that was built by the Benedictine monks from Little Malvern, who were granted the lands by Richard Tyrrell, 1st Baron of Castleknock, in 1185. The monks built their abbey on the site of an older Celtic monastery that was dedicated to St Brigid. It is believed that this site has been a Christian place of worship since the sixth century. The nearby well suggests that it may have been a place of pagan pre-Christian ritual as many Christian foundations were placed where people had been gathering for spiritual purposes.

The present church was built on the profile of the church in Beranger's painting between 1803 and 1810. A spire was added in 1864 in memory of the late James Hamilton, MP for County Dublin. The family would later be ennobled as Lords Holmpatrick. This spire was struck by lightning in 1957 and had to be dismantled. Strangely enough, the older church lost its spire in 1710 and Dean Swift, who was a friend of the vicar the Revd Thomas Walls, wrote a little ditty about it.

The Revd Charles Proby, one of the vicars who served here, eloped in 1691 with a niece of Archbishop Marsh and married her in a tavern. At first the elderly prelate was enraged and reduced him to a curate and disinherited his niece. As time passed he later forgave them but was unable to find the will or document whereby he disinherited her in order to restore her inheritance. Archbishop Marsh was the founder of Marsh's Library adjacent to St Patrick's Cathedral and had secreted the document in one of the books. It is said that the prelate's ghost has been seen in an eternal search in that library for the misplaced document. It is not clear why he could not have just have written up another will retracting the previous one.

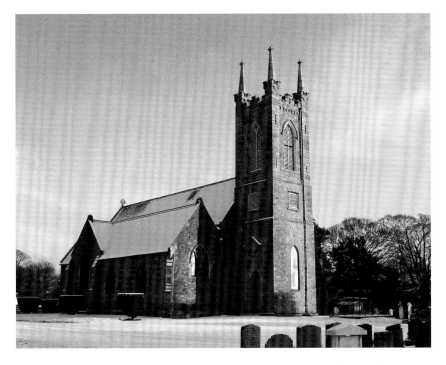

St Brigid's church, 2010, photograph by author. The present church of St Brigid's is a very pretty church and is a focal point in the village of Castleknock. In 1928 the Brooke family of Somerton presented a magnificent Harry Clarke stained-glass window of St George, St Hubert and St Luke as a memorial to their father George Frederick Brooke.

The churchyard is the last resting place for both Protestants and Catholics from the locality, including prominent local landowners and gentry.

Revd Ralph Sadlier, rector of Castleknock 1848-1903, photographer unknown. The Revd Sadlier was rector of Castleknock for fifty-five years and was a strong, forthright individual. His term of office coincided for a time with that of Fr Michael Dungan's, who was parish priest of St Brigid's Blanchardstown from 1836 to 1868.

There was a big controversy between the two clergymen concerning the religious education of children in Porterstown School and Abbotstown School. During a visit to Porterstown, Lord Eglington made a tart reference to RCs and bibles that reignited the row.

It was not until January 1965 that the rector of Castleknock and the parish priest of Blanchardstown joined together in public prayer when Canon Erberto Neil of Castleknock and Canon Morgan Crowe conducted a joint ecumenical service in the parish field.

Raymond Brooke, in his book *The Brimming River*, tells a story of an incident at divine service in St Brigid's, Castleknock. The congregation were awaiting the Revd Sadlier's entry to begin the service. The rector was unusually late and the worshippers were worrying about what was causing the delay. Amongst the congregation were the Holmpatrick, Guinness, and Brooke families and they were busy people with places to go and things to do.

After a while the vestry door opened slightly and the Revd Sadlier's head appeared around the door. He was clutching a bottle of altar wine in his hand. He enquired if someone could oblige with a corkscrew as the wine was necessary for the service. One member of the congregation was able to supply the necessary piece of equipment. It was of course Lord Iveagh of the Guinness brewing family.

Site of St Brigid's Well, Castleknock, photograph by author. The well was originally a little further to the southwest and the water was said to be noxious to the lower orders of life but excellent for higher mammals and humans. This well is close to the churchyard and wells close to churchyards are not conducive to good health; the cholera problem in Finglas in the 1800s was caused by one such well.

It is believed by many that the St Brigid's church site, where the Benedictine monks from Little Malvern, Worcestershire, founded an abbey in 1185, was originally the location of an older, possibly even pre-Christian religious site as the early Christian missionaries integrated the beliefs of the native Irish to facilitate their conversion. The proximity of the well to the church strengthens this argument as the Irish and other European peoples had a magical belief in the efficacy of wells as a source of cures. Most early Christian sites in Ireland are associated with holy wells. St Brigid, also known as St Bride, gave her name to many wells and places not only in Ireland but England and Scotland.

In fact, the cult of St Brigid spreads all over Western Europe. Strasbourg, Bruges, Cologne, London, northern Italy, Portugal, Spain, Switzerland and Sweden all have sites associated with the saint.

Many scholars believe that St Brigid's is syncretised with the pagan goddess Brighid. Similar to what happened in St Patrick's case, a fusion of different characters may have occurred and at this juncture it is unlikely we will discover an individual St Brigid.

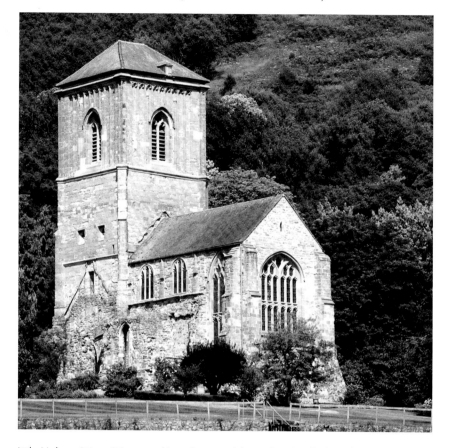

Little Malvern Priory, Worcestershire, photograph by author. Monks from the priory founded St Brigid's Abbey in Castleknock. The Anglican Little Malvern Priory and Little Malvern Court, a private manor house, was once the site of a famed monastic centre dating back to 1171. It was founded by two brothers, Jocelin and Edred, who were monks in the Benedictine Order, and it became a great centre of learning. William Langland, the first poet to write in English (as opposed to Anglo Saxon), was educated there.

The priory attracted the support of Gilbert de Clare Earl of Gloucester (a nephew of 'Strongbow' Earl of Pembroke). The de Clares were intermarried with the de Laceys and the Tyrrells.

In 1184 Richard Tyrrell, Baron of Castleknock, granted lands at Castleknock to the monks with the intention of founding a Benedictine Abbey. In 1215 Henry de Londres, Archbishop of Dublin consecrated the priory at Clonsilla, now St Mary's church, replacing the Irish abbey of St Mochta. These lands were also granted to the monks by the Tyrrell family along with a mill on the Liffey known as the Red Mill.

Unfortunately Little Malvern Priory and its monks became subject to criticism for various lapses and irregularities from the mother house at Great Malvern. This mission fell into decay and neglect and by the time King Henry VIII dissolved the monasteries there was little left in Little Malvern to dissolve.

It is now thriving Christian community worships in St Giles' Little Malvern Priory, encouraged by their pastor Canon Eric Knowles.

Former post office, Castleknock village, courtesy Tom Mongey. Michael Roche Breen built this post office, which was completed in 1900. Prior to that he was teaching in St Vincent's College until 1894, when there was a dispute between him and the college authorities. Breen was a supporter of Parnell and when the party split he continued to support the Parnellite faction of the Irish Party. He appeared on an election platform at a rally in Blanchardstown, much to the chagrin of the college authorities. The college authorities would have supported the status quo in terms of politics and Parnell's living arrangements with Katherine O'Shea, who was married to another man, were anathema to Church teaching. Breen's teaching career in Castleknock was no longer tenable.

Breen secured a teaching post in Mount St Joseph's, Roscrea. Either the authorities there were more liberal or were unaware of Breen's politics. It is thought that Breen was assisted by fellow members of Parnell's party in the setting-up of the post office. His wife, Nora Guiney Breen, was appointed postmistress and moved from Oak Cottage on Castleknock Road into the post office house. She lived and worked there until her death in 1923.

Her daughter, Mary Emmeline Breen, who was post office assistant, then took over the job until her resignation in 1981 at the ripe old age of 93. She gave more than fifty-six years of service to the Department of Posts and Telegraphs. It is probably one of the longest terms of service worked by a State employee. She died four years later, aged 97 years.

When Miss Breen retired she was succeeded by her assistant Miss Jane Meade. Miss Meade had commenced her employment in the post office in 1946. She in turn retired in 1993, aged 70. She closed the shop and post office and renamed the building 'Village House'. It is today a dental surgery.

Castleknock Celtic Soccer Team U14s, 1992. Front row, second from right, is a young Colin Farrell, photograph courtesy Tony Jordan, Castleknock Celtic. Castleknock Celtic was founded in 1987 by Tony Jordan, Tommy Moore and Tony Dalton. The first chairman was Pat Dempsey while Jim Geraghty was playing for one of the senior teams and managing a junior side.

They started off in the green in Laurel Lodge. It was still strewn with some of the debris from Brady's farmhouse and blocks of concrete and lengths of timber from the new houses being built on what was once Brady's farm.

The club grew out of an adult soccer club founded two years earlier, Laurel Lodge FC. When they decided to extend the club to juvenile footballers they renamed it Castleknock Celtic. Peter Mahon, who lives locally, was at the time managing St Francis FC and donated a set of jerseys to the emerging club. Pete would later take St Francis FC to an FAI final – the first time a non-league side reached an FAI cup final in fifty years.

Castleknock Celtic today caters for over 700 players and many players have gone on to play professional football.

The team shown in the photograph are, from right to left, back row: Billy Byrne, Ronan Forde, Barry Maguire (capped for Ireland 1992), Dermot Dalton, Enda Farrell, Paul Keane, Liam Breen. Front row: Mick Terry, Kevin Bradley, Alan Prior, David Byrne, Colin Farrell, Tommy Browne.

Colin Farrell went on to make his name as a famous Hollywood actor but he was good enough for a career in professional soccer. His dad Eamonn was no slouch at soccer either. He played for Shamrock Rovers and earned two League of Ireland XI caps. He made seven appearances in the European Clubs Cup.

Knockmaroon House, Castleknock, home to the Guinness brewing dynasty, c. 1890, courtesy Katie Bracken. The Guinness family were elevated to the peerage and the present Lord Moyne is Jonathan Bryan Guinness, 3rd Baron Moyne. He is the son of Bryan Guinness, 2nd Baron Moyne and Diana Mitford. They were divorced and Lady Diana married Oswald Mosley, leader of the British Union of Fascists. Bryan married Elizabeth Nelson in 1936.

Lord Moyne is a retired merchant banker. He was previously a journalist and was also a member of the Conservative Party and served in a prominent role in the Conservative Monday Club. He is based mostly in his English home. Kieran Guinness is the present owner of Knockmaroon and he lives there with his wife Vivienne Guinness, editor at the Lilliput Press. He is a half brother of the 3rd Baron Moyne.

Bryan Guinness, the 2nd Baron Moyne, was a novelist and a poet. He became vice-chairman of Guinness Brewery in 1949 and he was governor of the National Gallery from 1955. He died in 1992.

His father, the 1st Baron Moyne, was Walter Edward Guinness and his mother was Lady Evelyn Stuart. Walter Guinness was born in Dublin, possibly in Farmleigh, in 1880. He was the third son of the Earl of Iveagh who purchased the nearby Farmleigh Estate in 1873 and later purchased Knockmaroon Estate in November 1884 from Captain John T. Brinkley. He married Lady Evelyn Stuart in 1903 and moved into Knockmaroon House. At this time the family also used Farmleigh and spent much time at their Elveden Hall Estate in Suffolk.

Walter Edward Guinness fought in the Second Boer War, during which he was wounded, and in the First World War, during which he rose to the rank of lieutenant colonel. He was awarded the DSO with bar for personal bravery during action in France.

He was a member of the Conservative Party and served as an MP and on becoming a baron he served in the House of Lords and became Leader of the House. During the talks and negotiations leading to the Anglo Irish Treaty in 1921 he trimmed his sails from being a strong supporter of the Union to accepting the Free State. Ever the pragmatist, he described his change of policy saying that given the choice between 'a slippery slope and a precipice he would favour the slippery slope'. He served as British Minister for Agriculture from 1925-1929.

During the Second World War he served as Colonial Secretary and later as Deputy Resident Minister in Cairo. This latter position gave him effective control of a large part of Africa and the Middle East. He was assassinated by a militant Zionist group, 'The Stern Gang', in 1944.

The previous owners of Knockmaroon were the Brinkley family. Capt. John T. Brinkley served as a captain in the Prince of Wales North Staffordshire Regiment and was subsequently given the position of Chief Constable of Warwickshire – a post he held until his death. His father was Captain Walter Stephen Brinkley of the 11th Hussars. He was born in 1826 and died in Bath in 1884. His grandfather was the first Royal Astronomer of Ireland, the Rt Revd John Mortimer Brinkley DD (1763-1835), who later became Bishop of Cloyne. He resided at Dunsink Observatory and later at Cloyne Cathedral. He never lived at Knockmaroon.

Sir Henry Marsh sold the property to Walter Stephen Brinkley in 1853. Marsh was a young surgeon and physician. He rose to become president of the Royal College of Physicians and was also Queen Victoria's personal medical doctor. He was a direct descendant of Archbishop Marsh who founded the famous library beside St Patrick's Cathedral.

Sir Henry Marsh bought Knockmaroon from Henry Warren Darley around 1846. Darley was a barrister and a member of the Royal Dublin Society and we know from a deed of settlement that he was living there in 1838. It is thought that the house is older, maybe dating from 1815-20. The original house was much extended in 1905 and again in 1960. The photograph predates the 1905 works.

Henry Warren Darley's grandson helped in providing the stirring music for Patrick McCall's 'The Boys of Wexford', 'Kelly the Boy from Killane' and 'Boolavogue'. He was one of the founders of the Feis Ceoil and was the first musical director of the Abbey Theatre.

Lord Moyne's Stables, later transformed into luxurious apartments, painting by Eugene Kennedy. These beautifully appointed apartments are situated on the grounds of Knockmaroon Estate and are an example of how old buildings can be transformed for a different use without changing their essential fabric.

Farmleigh House, Castleknock, once home to the Guinness brewing dynasty, photograph by Andrew Lacey. Farmleigh probably derives its name from the Census of 1659 when Castleknock was enumerated as two separate townlands. The area around the church and village was referred to as the 'Churchtowne of Castleknocke' while the area around the castle was described as the 'Castle farme of Castleknocke'. The 6-inch OS Map of 1838 is the first time Farmley (*sic*) appears on a map.

Farmleigh House and its demesne of 78 acres was purchased by the Office of Public Works on behalf of the Irish Government in 1999 for use as premier accommodation for visiting dignitaries and guests of the nation. It was the intention that this beautiful residence would showcase the best in Irish furnishing, artwork and interior decoration while extending a traditional 'Céad Míle Fáilte'.

The house was not used much by the Guinness family since the death of Benjamin Guinness, the 3rd Earl Iveagh, in 1992. His son, Arthur Edward Rory Guinness, lives on his 22,486 acres Elveden Estate in Suffolk.

It was the 4th Earl's decision to part with the Farmleigh demesne and its acquisition by the Irish government was fortuitous as Lord Iveagh allowed furniture, paintings, sculptures and other items in the house including the magnificent library to be loaned to the State. The entire collection of the library was donated by the 4th Earl to Marsh's Library Dublin a couple of years ago.

Farmleigh was built in the late 1700s as a small Georgian house and was purchased in 1873 from John Childley Coote by Edward Cecil Guinness on his marriage to Adelaide Guinness (his third cousin) of the banking branch of the family. He carried out major construction and refurbishment of the house, including the extension of the house to the west and a third storey from 1881 to 1884. The architect responsible for the design was James Franklin Fuller (1832-1925). He had previously worked on St Anne's in Clontarf for Lord Ardilaun. A ballroom wing was added in 1896, the design of William Young (1843-1900). A new conservatory was added in 1901/1902 and the gardens were replanted with exotic species. The woodland area was planted with a variety of broadleaved trees that add to the beauty and wonder of Farmleigh Wood to this day.

Sir Cecil Edward Guinness was a great philanthropist, founding the Guinness Trust and spending £1 million in 1890 on slum clearance and housing projects. He founded the Iveagh Trust and started the largest urban renewal in early twentieth-century Dublin. He developed St Patrick's Park and built the Iveagh Market, enabling small stallholders to sell their produce protected from the elements. In 1913 he refused to be persuaded by other employers to lock-out workers in the Great Lock Out.

He was knighted Baron Iveagh in 1895, raised as Viscount Iveagh in 1905 and made Earl of Iveagh in 1919.

On his death in 1927, his son Rupert Guinness (1874-1967) became 2nd Earl Iveagh. Rupert was a Unionist MP and like his father he was a philanthropist, being generous to hospitals in Dublin. He was involved in the launching of the Guinness Book of Records along with the McWhirter twins Ross and Norris. His only son Arthur was killed by a V2 rocket while serving in Belgium in 1945. Rupert's grandson Benjamin (1937-1992) became 3rd Earl in 1967 on Rupert's death.

Benjamin was simultaneously a sitting member of the House of Lords in Westminster and a senator of the Irish Senate in Leinster House. He married Miranda Daphne Jane Smiley in 1963 but they divorced in 1984. Lady Miranda was a very knowledgeable gardener and did much to beautify the gardens and grounds of Farmleigh. Benjamin Guinness Lord Iveagh died at the relatively young age of 55 in 1992 and the present Lord Iveagh, Arthur Edmund Rory Guinness, inherited the title.

Farmleigh clock and watertower, photograph by Andrew Lacey. The tower held 8,183 litres of water and was build by Edward Cecil Guinness in 1880. The water for human consumption is pumped from a well close to the Liffey on the Palmerstown side and from the river for the livestock. The pump was powered by a turbine driven from a mile-long millrace that takes its water from the Liffey at the Wren's Nest weir.

The tower was designed by James Franklin Fuller and is 37 metres high (some sources tentatively attribute the design to Thomas H. Wyatt). Fuller was involved in the design, refurbishment and extension of Farmleigh at the time the tower was constructed; it therefore confirms the tower as his design.

The mechanism of the clock was installed by Sir Howard Grubb, who was famous for his design of precise astronomical instruments. Patrick Connolly was the stonemason, assisted by local craftsmen James Campbell, Patrick Murray and John Finnegan. The gravel and sand were supplied by Tracey's of the Lower Road who quarried it from the Sandpits in Diswellstown and dredged the Liffey for fine river sand. Mr Wilson, an employee of Guinness's James's Gate Brewery, was clerk of works on the job.

In 1885 few, if any, farmworkers or tradespeople carried watches. They depended on public clocks and church bells to give the time. It was not uncommon for agricultural workers to start at 6 a.m. and to finish work when they heard the 6 p.m. Angelus bell. We can be sure that following a gruelling day's work the chiming of the Angelus bell was a very welcome sound.

Priests' tombstones in the keep of Tyrrell's old castle in St Vincent's College grounds, Castleknock, photograph by Alan Halford. This atmospheric picture captures the mystery and magic of this ancient stronghold, a dún for Milesian chieftains, a fort used by Viking raiders and later an Anglo-Norman castle dominating the surrounding countryside.

There are about 2,500 centuries of Irish history associated with this remarkable national monument that predates the nearby city of Dublin. Part of the history of the hill dates back to a time when history and myth were indistinguishable, a time before the Ford of the Hurdles carried man and beast over the Liffey waters to a place that would come to be known as Baile Átha Cliath.

St Vincent's College is today in the busy Dublin suburb of Castleknock yet its immediate surroundings are still unchanged. The college is close to the woodlands of Farmleigh demesne and Knockmaroon demesne yet the busy M50 is a few hundred metres from the front gates. The college grounds are mostly playing fields yet the front lawn is grazed by cattle. The ruins of the old Norman castle are adjacent, surrounded by trees and shrubbery.

Lord Russell of Killowen, photograph courtesy Fr John Doyle CM, St Vincent's College, Castleknock. Charles Russell, Lord Russell of Killowen, was a student of Castleknock who reached the zenith of his legal career when he became Lord Chief Justice of England in 1894. It was one big step for an Irishman but an even bigger one for one that professed the Roman Catholic faith. He was the first Roman Catholic to hold the office since Sir Edward Saunders in 1559.

Lieutenant Colonel Reynolds VC, courtesy Fr John Doyle, CM. St Vincent's College. Lieutenant Colonel James Henry Reynolds, VC, RAMC was a former student of Castleknock College. He was awarded a Victoria Cross for gallantry at the siege of Rorke's Drift, Natal, South Africa in January 1879. He was a native of Kingstown (now Dún Laoghaire). He died, aged 88, in 1932.

6

CLONSILLA, ONGAR & PORTERSTOWN

The area around St Mary's church, Clonsilla, is particularly scenic and the canal bank makes for a lovely walk. Nearby Porterstown is another lovely area with the delightful St Mochta's church and the bright airy sports fields with a terrific view of the Dublin and Wicklow mountains.

Ongar is a brand new village built within the past few years but in design could be an old traditional Irish village. The surrounding housing estates are well planned and designed.

St Mary's, Clonsilla, painting by Eugene Kennedy. St Mary's church was built in 1845/1846. The church was consecrated in 1846 by Archbishop Richard Whately (Whately's great-great-grandson is the actor Kevin Whately of the *Inspector Morse* and *Lewis* TV series). The church tower was added in 1850. The church was enhanced by a gift of the bells from St Werburgh's church near Dublin Castle. The steeple of St Werburgh's overlooked the castle yard. The authorities became concerned that it may be used as a vantage point to direct rifle fire into the castle yard so Clonsilla got the bells. The church has a very fine stained-glass window of St Fiacre, the work of the eminent artist Evie Hone. It was installed in the church in 1935.

In 1907 a search was carried out in the churchyard by detectives and uniformed police for the stolen 'Irish Crown Jewels'. The jewels were actually regalia connected with the Order of St Patrick and consisted of a Grand Master's star, badges encrusted with emeralds, rubies and diamonds and gold collarettes. They would be worth about €5 million today. They were stolen from a safe in the aforementioned Dublin Castle. King Edward VII, who was sovereign of the order, was said to be livid. A clairvoyant engaged by the authorities said she could see them beside a gate in Clonsilla churchyard. According to the news reports of the time all the police found were 'dank nettles and cow parsley'.

St Mary's, Clonsilla, on a snowy afternoon, photograph by author. St Mary's was built in 1845/1846; however, the site has been a centre of Christianity since at least 1215. Henry de Londres, Archbishop of Dublin, consecrated the priory at Clonsilla founded by the Benedictine monks from Little Malvern. These were the same monks that founded the priory at Castleknock, now St Brigid's.

Clonsilla already had a chapel dedicated to St Mochta, a disciple of St Patrick, at Coolmine. It was known as the White Chapel of St Mochta and the priory at Clonsilla replaced the Celtic chapel. This chapel was in the lands to the rear of Coolmine Community School. It was described as being in a ruinous state in 1429 and not a trace of it remains apart from its name through the adjoining townland of Whitechapel. St Mochta is commemorated in the church of St Mochta's in nearby Porterstown.

Some members of the Luttrell family from Luttrellstown Castle are interred in the vaults as are members of the White family who purchased Luttrellstown.

As is the case at St Brigid's, the churchyard accommodates all faiths. Dr Patrick Fitzsimons Archbishop of Dublin from 1763-1769, who was born in Porterstown, is buried there just outside the front door of the church. He was the Roman Catholic Archbishop of Dublin and during his term of office the Penal Laws were still in existence but relaxed. Until the early 1960s, it was the custom when Catholic burials were taking place that the coffin would be rested on the archbishop's tombstone and prayers would be recited before going to the grave of the deceased.

Coolmine House, home to the Kirkpatrick family for generations, painting by Donal MacPolin, courtesy of Grainne Ui Chaomhanaigh, Priomhoide Scoil Oilibhéir. Coolmine House was demolished in the 1970s. Scoil Oilibhéir is built on the former site of Coolmine House.

According to the Down Survey of 1655 Sir Edward Bolton, an English Protestant, held the lands of Coolmine and Ringwellstown, consisting of 420 acres, a thatched house with two chimneys, a barn, a stable and several little cottages. Bolton, who was Chief Baron of the Exchequer, acquired the estate from the Earl of Thomond, who in turn had it from Walter Peppard. Peppard was granted ownership of the land after it had been confiscated from St Mary's Abbey, Dublin (not the Clonsilla priory) during the dissolution of the monasteries under King Henry VIII.

Alexander Kirkpatrick (1714-1791) of Drumcondra House purchased the house and estate of Coolmine from Robert Bolton Esq. in May 1780. He paid £14,500 for the property at the time, which was considered an expensive price. The Kirkpatrick clan were from Drumfrieshire in Scotland and one of the Kirkpatrick ancestors saved the life of King Robert the Bruce, making effective use of a dagger to dispatch the potential assassin. The family motto was 'I Make Sure', a reference to ensuring King Robert the Bruce's safety, and their emblem is a dagger. The Kirkpatricks came to Ireland with the army of King William of Orange in 1690 and were involved in the woollen trade and other agricultural business.

A Mr John Evans of Greystones purchased 111 acres of the estate in the late 1920s and over the years the remainder of the estate was sold. The Royal Canal Bridge near Coolmine railway station is called Kirkpatrick Bridge and Kirkpatrick Avenue and Drive are nearby. Other than that there is nothing left of their time in the area except these memories.

Clonsilla House, courtesy Fingal County Council. Consilla House was home to William Edward Hollowey Steeds from 1879 until his death in 1913. He was born in England and was a captain in the 7th Royal Lancashire Militia. He lived in various places in England before coming to Ireland to set up a stud farm. The move to Ireland may have been due to financial problems encountered in England.

In October 1887, Captain Hollowey's facility at Clonsilla featured in all the newspapers of the day as the scene of a horrific crime where thirty-eight horses were poisoned with arsenic, eighteen of whom died. Captain Steeds claimed £3,700 in compensation and was eventually awarded £3,000. Various suggestions were made as to the motive behind the poisoning. There was speculation that the Land League had become involved in an agrarian dispute with Steeds. Other sources pointed out that there was a row with an employee. An arson attack took place on the property in 1923, towards the end of the Civil War, with little damage.

Judge Wylie and his wife Ida bought the property in 1927. Ida died in 1950 after a long illness. Some years afterwards the judge went to live in the St Stephen's Green Club. He died in 1964. They are both buried in St Mary's churchyard, Clonsilla.

The house and its lands were sold for housing development. Unfortunately the house was destroyed by fire in the early 1970s.

All that remains of Clonsilla House demesne is a Tudor-style gate lodge that doubled as a farrier's forge. The house, now private property, has inscribed on its walls 'WEHS 1901', simply the initials of William Edward Hollowey Steeds and the year it was built.

Judge William Evelyn Wylie, the judge from Clonsilla who made history, photographer unknown. Clonsilla's legal eagle, mentioned in James Joyce's Ulysses, acted as prosecuting counsel for the government in the court-martials of the 1916 leaders, he was legal advisor to Dublin Castle prior to the Truce, a founding member of the Irish Red Cross, a High Court judge during the British administration and remained on the bench during the Free State period.

William Evelyn Wylie was born in Dublin in 1881, the son of a Presbyterian minister. During his time as a student at Trinity College he took up cycle racing. It was in relation to his participation in that emerging sport that earned him his mention in Ulysses.

In 1915 he joined the Territorial Army and was attached to the Officer Training corps (OTC) in Trinity College.

When the Easter Rising broke out he was on holiday in the south of Ireland. On his return to Dublin, he telephoned the OTC in Trinity and was told to report to Pembroke town hall, where the Inniskilling Fusiliers were posted. Major Armstrong of that regiment asked him what he did for a living. When Wylie replied that he was a barrister he was whisked off to the Provost Marshal and given the job of interviewing the republican prisoners. He was later asked to report to General Byrne who engaged his services in the prosecution of the 1916 leaders.

In the subsequent court-martials he seems to have formed a high respect for the men who appeared before the court, particularly Pearse. He mentions in his memoir that General Blackadder suggested that the names printed on the Easter Proclamation could be used as proof that the signatories' were responsible for the organisation of the rebellion. Wylie advised that the names were not signed but merely printed on the document and that was not proof. Wylie was also struck by the demeanour of Thomas Clarke, who did not offer any defence, who was cool and forthright throughout his court marital and came across as being a brave and kindly man. Wylie attempted to postpone Connolly's court martial on account of Connolly's injuries but the court did not agree. He was subsequently withdrawn or, as is more likely, withdrew as prosecution counsel in Connolly's trial.

Writing of de Valera, Wylie maintained that his American citizenship was not mentioned during his court martial. He recalls General Maxwell showing him Asquith's telegram curtailing the executions and enquired who was next on the list. 'Somebody called de Valera, sir,' replied Wylie.

'I wonder is he likely to make trouble in the future?' asked Maxwell.

'I wouldn't think so, sir. I don't think he is important enough,' answered Wylie. A lifetime later Wylie remarked, 'I told the truth, but my God, I was far off the mark.'

Returning to private practice after the court martial, Wylie once again took up work on behalf of the government in 1919 as Law Adviser under Lord French. This period saw the stepping-up of the War of Independence. It was also the time of the Black and Tans, ambushes and reprisals such as burning and looting by forces of the State.

It was a problematic time for Wylie, who was a liberal Unionist and a fair-minded and honest man who had come to realise that a certain measure of independence should be conceded. He spoke out against the Black and Tans and the policy of official reprisals.

By August 1920, Wylie had become prominent in a move towards conciliation with the support of General Macready and several others in the Dublin Castle administration, including Andrew Cope; however, at this time Lloyd George was intent on introducing coercion measures, i.e. the Law and Order Bill. Wylie saw this as military coercion and so he resigned from office in protest. Later that year he was appointed as a High Court judge.

Following the formation of the Irish Free State, Wylie received the seal of office for a second time as a senior judge but this time it was from the Executive Council of Saorstát Éireann. He held this office, along with the position of Judicial Commissioner of the Irish Land Commission, until 1936. He was highly influential and his advice was eagerly valued by many interests in the new Free State.

Through his influence with the Royal Dublin Society he assisted in the transfer of the society's Leinster House to the new State for Dáil and Seanad Éireann.

A keen horseman and supporter of equestrian sports, he served as a steward of the Irish Turf Club and on the National Hunt Steeplechase Committee. He was instrumental in enhancing the international prestige of the Dublin Horse Show along with Lord Holmpatrick, his near neighbour, and Captain F. Barton. He gave much time in the formation of the Irish Army's Equitation School in McKee Barracks.

Wylie was one of the founding members of the society and general council of the Irish Red Cross and served on it with Eamonn Ceannt's widow Aine. Ceannt was one of the executed 1916 leaders whom he prosecuted. Later on Eamonn Ceannt's brother became Wylie's registrar in the Land Commission. Helena Moloney, of Cumann na mBan, also served with Wylie on the Red Cross council.

In all his interaction with the many historic figures of the time he possibly had more conflict with Eamon de Valera than any other. However, in the autumn of his life it was 'de Valera who telephoned him several times with good wishes and appreciation of his great work for Ireland.'

Only one personality of the time seems to draw ire from Wylie's pen – in an uncharacteristic remark he said 'that having made a fool of himself on the Boundary Commission negotiations, Eoin MacNeill remained in the comparative obscurity for which he was admirably suited.'

The Deep Sinking, Royal Canal, Clonsilla, photograph by Eugene Kennedy. Tragedy occurred on the Royal Canal near Porterstown School House on 25 November 1845. Sixteen people were drowned when a canal barge struck a projection from the bank at a spot called McGovern's Rocks. There was panic amongst the passengers who, in the process of fleeing the sinking boat, further destabilised it, which resulted in a greater loss of life. The boat was being steered by a passenger – the normal steersman had absented himself and the captain was not in effective command. Fr Michael Dungan PP, when alerted of the tragedy, galloped along the dark narrow lands and the precipitous canal towpath to give the victims the last rites.

One of the passengers, Private Jessop of the 8th Hussars, was conspicuous in his efforts to save the lives of as many as he could and was lauded in the newspapers for his actions.

Porterstown National School, photograph by Eugene Kennedy. This building was built in 1853 by James Kennedy, a licensed vintner with premises in Capel Street. Kennedy and his brother Charles gave a suit of clothes to every boy with 100 per cent attendance in a year. Absenteeism was rife in Victorian Ireland. Children were taken out of school regularly by parents to help with the harvest and for sowing or ploughing. Girls were kept at home to help with the housework.

Many homes were steeped in poverty and that in turn introduced ailments and illness. There were no labour-saving devices and hunger and cold were an everyday reality. Families could not cope and children were required to help out at home and on the land.

The building itself has an eerie appearance and ghost stores are told about it. However, many local people went to school there and have happy memories of their schooldays. The school was an ordinary national school with two doors – one for the boys and one for the girls. It served the locality well until it closed down in 1962.

Canal Bank at Callaghan Bridge, Clonsilla, photograph by author. The canal here is a long stretch of level water; there are no locks from the 12th Lock at Talbot Bridge until Deey Bridge, Maynooth, a distance of 19 kilometres.

The bridge over the canal was originally called Carhampton Bridge after Henry Lawes Luttrell, 2nd Earl of Carhampton who held that title. He was director of the Royal Canal Company and lived in nearby Luttrellstown Castle. He carried out many atrocities before, during and after the 1798 Rebellion. Some historians believe his atrocities did more to provoke rather than suppress the nascent rebellion. The name of the bridge was changed to that of a popular local landowner because of the hatred for Henry Lawes Luttrell.

During the First World War the locality supplied a vast number of horses to the War Office. Horses were used by mounted cavalry units and also for pulling heavy artillery pieces and carts. A field on the far side of the bridge was used as a paddock for horses to be corralled. A purchasing officer would sit behind a table in the centre of the field flanked by a pay clerk. The horses would be paraded past the table and put through their paces, usually by local man Mr Smith. The horses purchased would then be loaded onto the train at Clonsilla station and brought to the North Wall and shipped to England.

St Mary's church, Clonsilla, photograph by Eugene Kennedy. St Mary's church is one of the prettiest churches in County Dublin. Its churchyard is well kept and the flowering cherry trees are particularly beautiful in spring.

The name Clonsilla comes from the Irish *Cluain Saileach*, 'the sally meadow.' *Saileach* is derived from the Latin word for willow, *salix*. This Latin word gives, in its corrupted form 'sally', the alternative English word for that particular tree. The monks were great believers in the efficacy of herbal potions and poultices in the treatment of illness. Most monastery gardens grew an assortment of medicinal plants, including willow.

Willow leaves and bark were used to treat certain conditions. It is known that people chewed the bark and leaves of willow to help relieve pain. Salicylic acid, used in the manufacture of aspirin, and wintergreen are both derived from sally bushes and the spirea plant.

Willows were also used to make baskets and today they are grown for use as wood pellets in ovens.

Ongar House, courtesy Olivia Leonard, 'The Past and the Present Blanchardstown and Surrounding Areas', Online History Group. Ongar House was originally called Hansfield House after the Hon. Hans Blackwood who owned the house and lands in the late 1700s early 1800s. The Blackwoods were barons of Dufferin and Ava but there is little information on their stay in Ongar. They were mainly based at Killyleagh, County Down.

Thomas Williams owned the house in the mid-1800s. He sold it to Patrick Bobbett, the descendant of a French mariner who was wrecked off the Dublin coast and settled in Dublin. Bobbett had a thriving market garden business. Patrick's son, William Bobbett, inherited Hansfield in 1886. William Bobbett was active in St Mochta's parish and donated £100 towards the building of St Mochta's church in 1890 – a substantial amount for the time.

Colonel Arthur Pollock bought Hansfield in 1926 and changed the name to Ongar after a town in Essex. Prince Aly Khan purchased the property in 1943. His wife, the Hollywood star Rita Hayworth, put a twinkle in the eyes of many local men on her frequent visits to Ongar. Unfortunately Prince Aly Khan died in a motor accident in Paris in 1960.

The next owner was an American businessman, Donal Strahelm, who bought the property after Aly Khan's death. Then a Mayo man, Phil Sweeney, had the property until 1989 when he sold it to a subsidiary of Monarch Properties who sold it on to Manor Park home builders in 1995.

Manor Park designed a brand new village using the house as a centrepiece. The village is an architectural gem and the Manor Park must be praised for creating such a picturesque traditional Irish village in the midst of their large housing development.

Dr John Thomas Troy, Archbishop of Dublin 1786-1823, painting by Thomas Clement Thompson, courtesy the National Gallery of Ireland. Dr Troy was born in Annfield House Porterstown. His term of office was a difficult time for Roman Catholics and even more so for members of their clergy. The Penal Laws were at times fully or partially implemented so an immense degree of tact and diplomacy was necessary.

The government included Lords Castlereagh, Clare and Clonmel who were prejudiced against the Roman Catholic religion and its adherents; curiously Lord Clare's father was born into the Catholic faith and only left because the Penal Laws prevented his admission to the Bar. This was a time of revolutionary fervour, firstly in America and later France. Other countries of continental Europe followed suit. Ireland was influenced by these events; the United Irishmen were planning rebellion and the White Boys, the Defenders, the Orange Order and other belligerent groups were agitated. During the 1798 Rising that followed atrocities were committed by both sides.

Dr Troy had come to an agreement with the British Government, which culminated in the foundation of Maynooth College in 1795. This college was to provide for the education of seminarians to the priesthood in Ireland and would be funded by State monies. The quid pro quo was that the British Government would have a say and a veto in the appointment of Roman Catholic bishops in Ireland.

The French Revolution was a time of persecution for the Roman Catholic Church. Dr Troy, fearing a similar revolution in Ireland, co-operated with the government while at the same time seeking concessions for his flock. The British Government suspected that priests educated on the continent might introduce revolutionary ideas into the country so concluded that it was far better to train them in Maynooth. Dr Troy was from gentry stock and was conservative by nature – as Bishop of Ossory he had ordered a day of prayer and fasting to ensure that the American colonists would not achieve their independence. Troy thought that keeping a low profile was the safest option for the Catholic population. Troy was not politically inclined and had little sympathy for Irish nationalism; he was a churchman first and last. It was said that Maynooth Seminary was worth more to King George III than several regiments of cavalry. Dr Troy, however, made entreaties on behalf of individual prisoners and advised a policy of restraint following the defeat of the insurgents in 1798.

With all that he was still distrusted. Lord Chancellor Redesdale said 'Maynooth vomits out priests ten times worse than ever came from the Spanish colleges. Redesdale made this outburst when Dr Troy was urging his flock to 'Fear God, honour the King, obey and respect your superiors of every description,' and while he was describing the handful of his clergy that were involved in the 1798 Rebellion as 'the very faeces of the Church.'

Troy was in favour of the Act of Union and encouraged the Irish hierarchy to row in behind him, believing that Prime Minister Pitt would deliver Catholic emancipation. Incredibly, the Orange Order disapproved of the Act of Union with scores of lodges passing resolutions to that effect.

When the Act of Union was passed, King George III refused to sign the bill granting emancipation, asserting that it would violate his Coronation Oath and Pitt resigned.

The Penal Laws and the implementation of them were eventually relaxed over a period of years until Catholic emancipation was introduced in 1829.

An interesting fact is that in 1815, at the laying of the foundation stone of the Pro-Cathedral, the Dean of Christchurch, prominent Dissenters, Quakers and Orangemen were in attendance; the Guinnesses and Daniel O'Connell were also present.

Dr Troy died on 11 May 1823. As the Pro-Cathedral was unfinished, he was not interred there until 1825. Dr Troy was the last Catholic archbishop to retain the old feudal title of baron in his description. His many pieces of plate have a baron's coronet added to the ecclesiastical hat, and there are tassels on his coat of arms.

The Troy's family tomb is in the long-disused local graveyard of Caeveen, now in the grounds of the National Sports Campus. His brother, Walter Troy, appears to have been the last of the family to be interred there.

St Mochta's church, Porterstown, photograph by author. The church of St Mochta's was built as a chapel of ease for St Brigid's, Blanchardstown, in 1890. The land for the church was gifted to the parish by a local landowner, James Warren of Astagob. His descendants live in the parish to this day. The Warren family also provided the land for St Brigid's, the parish church, in 1835.

This new chapel replaced an older chapel built by local landlord Luke White in 1838 in Kellystown. The site of this chapel was later used as the Scouts' den. An earlier chapel was located near Pound Hill, Luttrellstown.

St Mochta (c. 455-c. 535) was a disciple of St Patrick and was consecrated as Abbot Bishop of Louth in Rome. St Mochta was born in Britain and was brought to Ireland as a child with his parents who settled here. He was the founder of the White Chapel of Coolmine – an abbey that was later taken in charge by the Benedictine monks from Little Malvern in the twelfth century. The location of the abbey was transferred to where St Mary's church, Clonsilla, stands.

The church of St Mochta's is very beautiful and is the design of Williams Hague, FRIA. The foundation stone was laid by Archbishop Walsh, assisted by the Very Revd Michael Donovan, parish priest in Blanchardstown, and Revd James William CC, Porterstown. The total budget for the building was £20,000. Today the church is a popular venue for weddings and it is said that the acoustics of the church are of remarkable quality. Concerts in aid of local charities, particularly for St Francis Hospice, have been held in the church with great success.

Rita Hayworth and Aly Khan – once owners of Ongar Stud and frequent visitors to the locality, photographer unknown. Rita Hayworth has a road on the Ongar estate named after her.

7

DISWELLSTOWN AND SOMERTON

Diswellstown and Somerton are two delightful small townlands overlooking the River Liffey near Strawberry Beds. Despite their small size they have an exciting history, mainly due to some of the fascinating characters that lived there. Both have retained their rustic beauty to this day and are very scenic.

The Castleknock Hotel & Country Club is located in Somerton and attracts visitors from home and abroad. The fine golf course adjacent to the hotel is much appreciated by golfers who enjoy a challenging game and Castleknock Hurling & Football Club has a wonderful facility for Gaelic games in Somerton Lane.

Sandpit Cottages, Diswellstown, photograph by author. On the high road to Lucan via Porterstown (the lower road is the road alongside the Liffey through Strawberry Beds) we see the picturesque Sandpit Cottages at Diswellstown with their distinctive blue and white colours. The name of the cottages comes from their proximity to an earlier sandpit – a source of sand and gravel for generations.

The cottages were built for workers on Lord Moyne's Knockmaroon estate. This area featured a couple of years back standing in for the north of England in the late 1950s and early 1960s for the *George Gently* TV series.

When Lord Moyne, a member of the Guinness brewing family, was elevated to the peerage, the story goes, two other earls were having a drink at the bar. The door opened and Lord Moyne joined some company at the other end of the bar. One of the earls nudged his companion saying 'Who's 'e then?' and the other replied, without missing a beat, 'Oh! Moyne's a Guinness'.

Tommy Bracken, local bard and poet with Arkle, courtesy Katie Bracken. Tommy Bracken lived in the Sandpit Cottages as a tenant of Bryan Guinness Lord Moyne. They would often meet and talk of poetry when Lord Moyne was staying in Knockmaroon. Lord Moyne was a poet in the classical tradition yet a common love of poetry knew no boundaries.

Tommy came from an ancient bardic tradition. He put the news of the day into rhyme. He wrote of football and hurling matches, of Stephen Roche winning the Tour de France. He wrote of emigrants and navvies and of the helicopter escape from Mountjoy Prison but his favourite topic was his beloved Arkle, possibly the best racehorse ever. In his 'Farewell Arkle', written as an obituary on the death of this gallant racehorse, he touched hearts.

This is Tommy's poem, courtesy of his sister Katie Bracken:

FAREWELL ARKLE

You ran and you jumped like a bird on the wing
And in centuries from now they'll still call you king.
If they can travel through time, they'll go back in force
To the year 'sixty-four' at Cheltenham Race Course.

They'll see a large crowd standing so tense
As you challenge Mill House at the second last fence.
They'll be glad to be there for that memorable day
As they see you land first and go racing away.

Into history and glory as loud the cheer rends
Your first Gold Cup victory by an easy five lengths
And for the Gallagher Gold Cup for Sandown they'll head
As you carry top weight pulling hard for your head.

And the crowd will be roaring as you jump the last first
And go streaking away with an electrifying burst.
They'll see all your great victories carrying top weight
But at Kempton Park they'll be cursing cruel fate.

Because that was the day in the 'George the Fifth' chase
That you raced on three legs, t'was your very last race.
Ah, not alone had you greatness but true courage as well
You won all the top chases and never once fell.

But never again on a racecourse if for centuries we wait
Will we see your equal Bold Arkle the Great.
So from all of us now who loved you so well
We'll remember you always Arkle ... Farewell.

Every Friday night Tommy used to hop the bus into town and go from pub to pub selling his latest poem or ballad that he had run off earlier in the day on a Roneo Gestetner. Many's the time, with a pint in one hand and a sixpenny bit in the other, I would purchase one of Tommy's renditions from the bard himself and muse over the contents while enjoying a pint of Lord Moyne's best. Tommy was our very own northside Zozimus from the Sandpits in Castleknock.

Thomas Bracken, author of the national anthem of New Zealand, photograph courtesy Katie Bracken. The Bracken family of Sandpit Cottages were related to Thomas Bracken. He was born on 21 December 1843 near Clonee, County Meath, and wrote many poems after he emigrated to Australia before eventually settling in New Zealand. Someone in County Monaghan mistakenly read his birthplace as Clones instead of Clonee, which resulted in the erection of a plaque on the public library in Clones, County Monaghan, celebrating Bracken's birth. If Tommy was alive no doubt he would have penned a humorous ditty in response. The Bracken family have been generous benefactors to the new St Francis Hospice in Blanchardstown.

Bryan Guinness, 2nd Lord Moyne, courtesy Katie Bracken. Lord Moyne was an author and poet (see Knockmaroon House, p. 109). He came from a classical background in poetry; however, his love of traditional Irish rhyme led him to write this beautiful poem in 1936.

THE PRETTY GIRL MILKING THE COWS

She was pale as a lily
And as red as a rose
And her hair was as black
As the wings of the crows.

The morning has spangled
The cobwebs of silk;
And there gleamed on her fingers
The pearls of the milk.

My pony impatiently
Bore me away
But I carried her with me
All the bright day.

(From *On a Ledge: New & Selected Poems* (Lilliput Press, 1992),
courtesy Antony Farrell, Lilliput Press)

The Glen, Diswellstown, photograph by author. Across the road from the Sandpit Cottages is the lovely woodland path leading down to the River Liffey through the Glen.

About forty years ago the Glen was quarried by Harris's for sand. Nature returned to reclaim it when the quarry closed down. It is now a delightful glen with a small stream tumbling down to meet the Liffey. Many local people are unaware of this beauty spot on their doorstep. Some locals say the stream is called the River Dis. However, my sources suggest it was made up by a pupil doing a project on folklore in the 1930s. So what? This is how places get names.

The Deuswell family bought 578 acres of land from Baron Tyrrell in the thirteenth century, lending their name to Diswellstown.

Up the road, heading towards Luttrellstown, is the Ragwell. It was said to have a cure for complaints of the eyes. The hawthorn bush associated with the well was burnt unintentionally by travellers who lit a fire for cooking a meal there many years ago. Today the well is covered with a lid over which local people laid a flowerbed. This spot is particularly beautiful in spring, when primroses herald the arrival of the new season with their eye-catching display of colour providing a tonic for the eyes, as the well did in past years.

Oatlands House, Diswellstown, photographer unknown. Oatlands House and grounds are on the Porterstown Road, just past the Ragwell near the new playing fields of Castleknock Hurling & Football Club.

Oatlands was home to the Godley family in 1837 according to the *Lewis Topographical Dictionary*. One of the Godley family served as a vicar in St Brigid's Castleknock from 1764 to 1767. Lt Col Hill lived there in the 1850s and '60s, followed by Capt. Leslie Martin of Her Majesty's 12th Royal Lancers, who lived there in the 1880s. The Koenig family from Germany, who later moved to Castlemount (or Schloss Berg as they called it), resided there in 1914 and later in the 1940s one John A. Nicholson lived there. Other occupants included members of the Guinness family. However, one of the most interesting occupants was Col Sir Francis Fitzgerald Chamberlain KCB, Inspector General of the Royal Irish Constabulary from 1900 to 1914.

Sir Neville Francis Fitzgerald Chamberlain, painting unattributed. Sir Neville Francis Fitzgerald Chamberlain was a distant relative of the Chamberlain family that included Neville Chamberlain, Prime Minister of Britain at the outbreak of the Second World War.

Colonel Chamberlain was inspector general of the RIC during the 1916 Rising and oddly disregarded reports from British Naval Intelligence and other sources about the impending insurrection, leaving the RIC and British military totally unprepared for an armed rebellion in Ireland. Most of the British high command in Ireland were enjoying the Fairyhouse Races on Easter Monday when the Rising began and so 'the second city of the Empire' fell into the hands of the rebels for one week.

Chamberlain was relieved of his office in August of that year and, to quote his own words, 'retired to a life of hunting, shooting and fishing' until his death in 1944. However, in his earlier life, while serving with the 11th Devon Regiment in India, he devised the game of snooker. While posted in Jubbulpore (now Jabalpul) between 1874 and 1876 as a young subaltern he played a lot of billiards, which was a popular pastime with most young officers of the time. Jubbulpore was a quiet station and, with plenty of time on his hands, the young Chamberlain invented the game as an alternative to billiards.

On his next posting Chamberlain's service became a little more eventful and a lot more dangerous. He was wounded in the Afghan War while serving with the Central Indian Forces. He remained there until he recovered from his ordeal he then served in the Burma Campaign and later on travelled to South Africa, where he was private secretary to Lord Roberts during the Boer War.

Diswellstown House, courtesy Jeremy Kelly, Kelly Walsh Property Advisors. The Laidlaw family from Scotland relocated to Ireland in 1906 and bought Abbey Lodge, Carpenterstown, which they purchased from the Manley family. They bought Diswellstown House shortly afterwards and then went on to purchase Somerton in 1911 from the Brooke family.

Diswellstown House had a well with petrifying qualities. If one placed a stick in it the stick would appear to turn to stone, due to a similar chemical action as occurs when deposits are laid down in a kettle.

The Kennan family lived there before the Laidlaws. Thomas Kennan was a captain in the 34th Regiment of Foot. The family previously owned Annfield and Ashtown Lodge and were associated with the firm Mono Pumps. The Kennan's ironmongery supplied most of the ironwork in the Phoenix Park.

At one time, the Kennan's premises in Fishamble Street Dublin, was the Musik Hall, where George Fredrich Handel held the first performance of his majestic oratorio *The Messiah* on 1 October 1741.

There is an old walkway at the rear of Diswellstown House that many local people refer to as Canon's Lane, believing it to be an old Mass path. It is in fact Kennan's Lane and has nothing to do with senior clergy or military ordnance.

A family named O'Keeffe lived here also for a while.

Somerton House, courtesy Patrick Troy. Somerton House and its demesne is now the site of Castleknock Golf Club and Castleknock Hotel & Country Club. However, the fine house and immediate grounds are in private ownership. The late Phil Monahan, of Monarch Properties fame, purchased the house and demesne in 1988. Phil Monahan died in November 2012 but his family are still in residence.

The demesne's previous occupants were the Laidlaw family, who purchased it from the Brooke family in 1911. The Brooke family had bought it in 1830, having leased the property for some years from a Councillor Dunne. The *Lewis Topographical Directory* of 1837 has R. Manders as the occupant in 1837. As the Brookes also resided from time to time at their demesne near Coolgreany, County Wexford, it is possible that they let the house to R. Manders Esq.

Over the years the demesne has had a series of name changes. The original owner of the lands was Henry Lawes Luttrell, 2nd Earl of Carhampton, who sold it off in 1808 before he sold off the balance of his lands to Luke White a few years later. Luttrell had given the name Somerton to these lands after a village of that name in Somerset, near Dunster Castle, the seat of the senior branch of the Luttrell family. William Duncan's Map of Dublin 1821 shows the demesne as Airfield. The Brooke family reverted to the older name but spelt it as Summerton; the Laidlaws changed it to Somerton.

Coincidentally, the Guinness family had an airfield about half a mile away in the 1930s. It was closed in 1942 for security reasons but not before a Lysander aircraft of the Irish Army Flying Corps crash-landed that same year.

From 1911 until the 1970s the house and demesne of Somerton and the house and lands of Abbey Lodge Carpenterstown and Diswellstown House and lands were owned in their entirety by the Laidlaw family. Their stud farm was based at Abbey Lodge and two Grand National winners and a Derby winner were born there.

Raymond F. Brooke (1885-1964), author of *The Brimming River* and Grand Master of The Ancient Free and Accepted Masons of Ireland, photographer unknown. Raymond Brooke was descended from Captain Basil Brooke (1567-1633), who was awarded lands in Donegal for military service to the Crown. His descendants later transferred to Colebrook, County Fermanagh, having been awarded the lands of the McMahon and Maguire clans, which had been forfeited by the Crown. This family would later include Sir Basil Brooke, one time Premier of Northern Ireland and his uncle, Field Marshal Viscount Alan Brooke, foremost military advisor to Churchill during the Second World War.

The southern Brookes derived their fortune from land, banking and, latterly, the wine trade while continuing on a strong tradition of military service to the Crown. Their entry into business was frowned on by their more haughty Fermanagh relations as the army, law and the Church were the only professions deemed to be acceptable to gentry. The Fermanagh Brookes not only looked down on their relatives that were 'in trade', one of their number, Sir Basil Stanlake Brooke, 1st Viscount Brookeborough, former Premier of Northern Ireland, was a notorious bigot who said he would not employ Roman Catholics on his estate and advised others not to have one about the place. It was reported that during a Commonwealth conference he buttonholed Joseph Lyons, the Australian Premier, and enquired as to what percentage of the Australian population were Roman Catholics. When Lyons responded that it was in the region of 25 per cent Brookborough harrumphed, 'Watch them, they're disloyal and breed like bl—y rabbits'. Lyons was a Catholic and the father of twelve children.

Raymond F. Brooke's father had an estate at Coolgreany, County Wexford, where a series of notorious evictions took place in 1887. One of those evicted was a bedridden 80-year-old woman. The tenants were engaged in a protest against excessive rents with the support of the Land League. During the eviction one of the bailiffs killed a protestor. He was charged with murder but acquitted. The Brookes did not have difficulty with their Castleknock tenantry but the baronet's remark that the people in the gate lodges were not entitled to eat once a week the fare he enjoyed every day is indicative of a particular mindset. Raymond F. Brooke would not appear to have shared his father's views and seems to have been a liberal and kind man.

In his most enjoyable book, *The Brimming River*, Raymond F. Brooke tells of his schooldays in an English public school and his visits to Madam Tussaud's and the Aquarium. Among the attractions at the Aquarium was a circus of performing fleas. They pulled little cars and swung back and forth on tiny swings, and after the show the owner fed them from his own arm and placed them in cotton wool until their next performance.

The Brooke family had a certain cousin, Charlie from Avondale, who visited occasionally to play cricket; however, he was known to take the 'sulks' if the umpire's decision did not go his way. This was the famous Charles Stewart Parnell. The cricket pitch at Summerton is now the playing fields of Castleknock Hurling and Football Club.

The Brooke family were renowned for having one of the leading kennels of harriers in the country, the family being much celebrated within the hunting fraternity.

Letitia Marion Hamilton (1876-1964), daughter of Louisa Brooke, was a distinguished artist. A pupil of William Orpen, her painting 'Snowfall in Co. Down' is on permanent exhibition in the Hugh Lane Gallery of Modern Art. The Brookes' more local contribution to the arts is a magnificent Harry Clarke stained-glass window to St Brigid's church in Castleknock, which may be viewed to this day.

The White House after the Burning of Washington, artist unknown. Two members of Summerton's Brooke family were responsible for an outrageous act of arson. The War of 1812 between Britain and America was in its third year when a British force, under the command of Admiral Cockburn, attacked Washington. Colonels Arthur and Francis Brooke were leading a military raiding party and on entering an abandoned White House were somewhat delighted to come upon tables laden with sumptuous food in preparation for a banquet. The President of the United States, James Madison, had vacated the house in some haste the previous evening.

The Brooke brothers and entourage tucked into the food and returned the hospitality of their unwitting host by torching the building. The White House was badly burned; only a torrential rainstorm spared the building from complete destruction. The architect, James Hoban, a native of Callan, County Kilkenny, had the building completely renovated later, during which time the grey stonework was painted white to cover up the scorch marks – hence 'the White House'. Hoban's original design for the White House was influenced by Richard Cassell's Leinster House. The Rotunda Hospital was also based on Leinster House.

I should point out that although the Brooke brothers were of the Summerton branch of the family they did not live at Summerton.

The Suffragette Derby 1913, photographer unknown. The Laidlaws came from Scotland to settle here in 1906. The Laidlaws were originally iron-founders but later on moved into banking and eventually the manufacture of cotton thread. Their company, J. & P. Coates, became known worldwide for the quality of their thread.

T.K. Laidlaw was appointed High Sheriff in 1919 and was also a steward of the Irish Turf Club. He was the last person to be appointed to the Privy Council before Irish independence.

The English Derby winner in 1913, Aboyeur, was bred by T.K. Laidlaw at Abbey Lodge Stud. The site of this stud is now occupied by Cherry Lawn, Park, Drive and Avenue in Carpenterstown Park. This Derby became to be known as 'The Suffragette Derby', owing to Ms Emily Davison, a Suffragette who ran in front of the king's horse Anmer. She was so seriously injured that she died ten days later. The favourite in the race, Craganour, was disqualified for bumping. So, Aboyeur, the 100/1 chance won the race in the steward's room.

Most racing authorities believe that Craganour was the winner but his owner was Bower Ismay and he was a brother of Bruce Ismay, owner of the White Star Line whose flagship the Titanic sunk with the loss of 1,513 souls the previous year. Bruce Ismay was accused of taking a lifeboat place dressed as a woman at the time of the sinking. Apart from the opprobrium attaching to his alleged cowardice he was also *persona non grata* with some of the stewards owing to his extra-marital activities.

Mr Thomas K. Laidlaw, artist unknown, courtesy Frank O'Connor. Mr Laidlaw was the breeder of two winners of the Grand National and he also bred a Derby winner. He was very unlucky as he had sold them all before they achieved success. The Laidlaw family were popular in the locality and were generous to local charities and community causes. The Laidlaws' fields used to be easily identified as all their timber post fencing and gates were painted in an orange-brown paint.

The area of Castleknock, Blanchardstown and Clonsilla resounded to the thundering of horses' hooves from the various bloodstock stables in the area. William E.H. Steeds and later Judge Wylie in Clonsilla House, Michael Betagh followed by Sir Hugh Nugent in Lohunda House, Captain Delhurst in Clonsilla, and Maxie Arnott, also in Clonsilla, were all well-known and respected horse breeders and trainers.

Mr Joe Manley was a famous local rider and trainer. He had twenty-three winners in 1909 and won the Farmers' Race at Fairyhouse in April 1915. His father, Thomas Manley, was presented with a silver cup from Colonel Pope of the Dragoon Guards for his services to horse breeding in 1889. The Manley family were noted for their bloodstock and indeed supplied warhorses to the British Army for many years. They entertained King Edward VII at their Castleknock property in Laurel Lodge and staged a horse race for his entertainment at an area called the Gallops.

The Manleys later lived in Roselawn House, having sold their properties in Laurel Lodge and Carpenterstown. Roselawn House, long since demolished, was sited close to the junction of Roselawn Road with Castleknock Road, near Granard Bridge.

Somerton Cottage, Somerton Lane, courtesy Mary Eustace. This beautiful cottage, the home of May and Joe Tobin, was surrounded by flowers and the smell of the roses wafted the length of Somerton Lane. The bottom of Somerton Lane was known as the Woolly Corner as it was a spot where sheep were gathered prior to being driven in to the Dublin market. May Tobin's roses helped to counteract the smell from the sheep. Photographers came from all over to snap the postcard-pretty cottage on Somerton Lane.

8

THE LUTTRELL FAMILY AND LUTTRELLSTOWN CASTLE

The Luttrell family's presence in the area is longer than any other titled family. Their dynasty is so enmeshed in Irish history, both for good and bad, that I have devoted a section to the Luttrells and the other owners of the castle that came after them.

The early Luttrells seem to have enjoyed good relations with their fellow peers and their tenants. However, Henry Luttrell (1655-1714) changed all this and, with one or two exceptions, his descendants were unpopular in the area and did not have good relations with their fellow peers. Indeed, one member of the family was challenged to a duel by his father and rejected the challenge on the grounds that his father was not a gentleman.

The castle is, without doubt, one of the finest castles in Ireland and the grounds of the castle are particularly beautiful and very well kept.

Luttrellstown Castle, courtesy Luttrellstown Castle. The history of the Luttrell family in Ireland can be traced back to one Geoffrey Luttrell, who was appointed as a member of a royal commission by King John in 1204. Geoffrey was a supporter of King John from the time the king was Earl of Mortain. King John repaid his loyalty on his accession to the throne by including Luttrell as one of his ministers.

Indeed, there is a legend that King John stayed at Luttrell's castle. There are parts of the ancient fabric of the castle that could date back to the late thirteenth century. However, no documentary evidence has been discovered to date the present castle back that far or indeed to associate it with King John's visit to Ireland, which occurred in 1210. On balance, it is unlikely that John graced the castle with his presence.

There is a secret staircase embedded deep within the present house. It leads from what is fancifully named 'King John's Room' down well-trodden granite steps to the 'Van Stry Room' and on to a tiny dungeon or oubliette. It may be the remains of an old tower house built to defend the Pale that eventually became absorbed into the present building, as happened in the case of Ashtown Castle.

Luttrellstown Castle as we see it today is largely a rebuild dating back to the late 1700s or early 1800s. It is a Gothic revival with some Tudor influences but that does not detract from its strikingly beautiful appearance.

The Luttrells came to England with the army of William the Conqueror in 1066 and took part in the Battle of Hastings. They derived their surname from the French *l'outre,* meaning 'the otter', and incorporated an otter into their coat of arms.

As a reward for their loyalty, the Luttrells were awarded vast tracts of land in Somerset and Lincolnshire and owned the Isle of Lundy. Their family seat was Dunster Castle in Somerset.

Geoffrey Luttrell is said to have purchased his Luttrellstown Estate with 20 ounces of gold but he did not enjoy it for long as he died while on a royal mission to Pope Innocent III. This mission is thought to have been to secure the Pope's support in retracting the Magna Carta.

Between 1235 and 1246 Robert Luttrell was Lord Chancellor of Ireland and was also treasurer of St Patrick's Cathedral. In 1349 Simon Luttrell is recorded as having land and a mill near St Wolstan's in Lucan and fifty years later his son John was in possession of that property. From this John Luttrell the Luttrell line can be traced in unbroken succession.

The Luttrells married into the wealthy Anglo-Norman families that owned the rich rural lands surrounding the city, including the Plunketts, Bellews, Sarsfields, Travers, Fitz Lyons, Barnewells, Aylmers, Bathes, Dillons, Finglas, Seagraves, St Laurences, Fitzwilliams and Gouldings.

During the Reformation the Luttrells remained Roman Catholic but were not averse to sharing the spoils from the Dissolution of the Monasteries, and acquired the lands of Coolmine from St Mary's Abbey.

King James I imprisoned Sir Thomas Luttrell on two separate occasions for his involvement in the Irish Catholic cause. When Sir Thomas died in November 1634 he left his wife Alison Diswellstown House, twenty cows, three hundred sheep, six rams of the English breed, fifteen farm horses, four riding horses and a huge amount of silver plate. His younger children were left gold and silver coins of immense value and his eldest son Simon inherited the manor house and demesne at Luttrellstown.

Simon Luttrell sided with King Charles I against Parliament in the Civil War. At the end of hostilities Oliver Cromwell seized the lands of Luttrellstown and granted them to Colonel Hewson, Governor of Dublin. Hewson had started off in life as a humble shoemaker but rose through the ranks of Cromwell's New Model Army and sat on the parliamentary committee that condemned King Charles to death.

At this stage, Simon Luttrell was dead and his son Thomas, who was the lawful heir, was allowed by Hewson to live in the stables of his own castle, with his wife Barbara Seagrave.

The Down Survey initiated by Oliver Cromwell to assist in the transfer of lands to the supporters of Parliament shows: 'Symon Luttrell of Luttrellstown holding 834 acres of land in the Barony of Castleknock.'

At the Restoration of the monarchy in 1660 King Charles II returned Thomas Luttrell to his estate. At this period Luttrellstown was described as 'a great mansion house with twelve chimneys'.

During the war between King James II and William of Orange we find Simon and Henry Luttrell supporting King James. Simon stayed loyal to King James until his death in Europe in 1698. In contrast, Henry switched sides. Bear in mind that this was not a war between Britain and Ireland but between opposing claimants to the English throne and it has to be remembered that William was married to James's daughter Mary. Loyalty in that era was firstly to one's family or dynasty and afterwards, as was described in feudal terms, to one's liege lord. The concept of the nation state was still evolving and it was not unusual for brothers to take opposing sides in order that the family would preserve its estates come what may.

Henry performed well and fought bravely alongside his near neighbour Patrick Sarsfield of Lucan when he took Sligo and conducted himself well at the Battle of the Boyne. However, he withdrew his regiment of cavalry at a crucial stage in the Battle of Aughrim.

At the Siege of Limerick he was court-martialled for treachery as he was believed to be in communication with the Williamite forces. General Ginkel, commander of the Williamite forces, became aware of Luttrell's plight and sent a message across the lines to say that if one hair of Luttrell's head was harmed he would execute every Irish officer in his custody. It appears that his near neighbour and relative through marriage Patrick Sarsfield spoke up for him. As the war had reached its last stages and there was no prospect of victory for the Jacobite side there was probably no point in exacting revenge as it could affect the treaty negotiations.

MAGUIRE S

Henry Luttrell the Traitor (1655-1717), painting by Henry Brocas, courtesy National Library of Ireland. The description of Henry Luttrell as a traitor is probably correct as he did betray King James but only when he saw no hope of winning and James had fled and was safe in France. His brother Simon had gone with King James so were the Luttrells hedging their bets to ensure their properties would stay in the family? Maybe he should have more accurately been called Henry the Pragmatist. Neither side in that war were fighting for Ireland.

After the siege of Limerick, Col Henry Luttrell returned to his Luttrellstown estate, transferring his allegiance to King William of Orange. Henry Luttrell was notorious for his debauchery and was universally detested. It was also said locally that he had a mill erected on the Liffey near Luttrellstown in one night owing to the assistance of his Satanic Majesty.

Finally, fate caught up with Henry Luttrell and he was fatally wounded by a pistol shot in the autumn of 1717 while returning to his city residence from Lucas Coffee House on Cork Hill in a sedan chair. No one was ever apprehended for the killing as he had so many enemies with so many motives that it was impossible to identify a main suspect out of so many.

Such was the hatred that he personally engendered that eighty-one years after his death his tomb was broken open during the 1798 Rebellion by local people in Clonsilla. His remains were removed and a pickaxe was used to smash his skull.

The Devil's Mill, River Liffey, near Luttrellstown, 1792, drawing by Jonathan Fisher (1740-1809). There are many far-fetched stories about how Henry Luttrell came to strike a deal with the Devil to get him to build a mill on the River Liffey adjoining his demesne in one night. One piece of local folklore tells us that he promised his soul to the Devil in exchange for having the mill built in one night. The contract was agreed and many years later the Devil arrived at Luttrell's club to collect. The brave young bucks scattered in all directions at the sight of the Devil, crushing each other in their rush to get out the door. Luttrell was the last one left and was fleeing towards the door when he spotted his own flickering shadow reflected on the wall as he passed a large candle. He tricked the Devil by pointing at the shadow while shouting out, 'There he is!' The Devil grabbed the shadow and Luttrell escaped and since then no descendant of Henry Luttrell casts a shadow.

The mill was later reconstructed as Anna Liffey Mill in 1820 and was acquired in 1859 by Joseph Shackleton of the famous milling family of that name. The family included in their number the noted explorer Henry Shackleton. The mill ceased production in 1998. The mill provided employment for many local people. The Shackletons were described as benevolent employers and, apart from an incident during the 1913 Lockout, industrial relations were excellent.

The Hell Fire Club, painting by James Worsdale, courtesy National Gallery of Ireland. The painting depicts, from left to right: Henry Barry, 4th Lord Santry; Col Clements; Col Ponsonby; Col St George and Simon Luttrell. This Simon Luttrell (1713-1787) is Henry Luttrell's son, not his brother Simon. The bottle on the table contains scaltheen, a concoction of whiskey and melted butter, a favourite tipple of club members.

Simon inherited the property and title on his father's death. As a young man he was given the nickname the King of Hell, due to his debauched lifestyle. He married a very wealthy heiress, Judith Maria Lawes daughter of Sir Nicholas Lawes, Governor of Jamaica. He was raised to the peerage as 1st Earl of Carhampton. He was a prominent member of the Hell Fire Club. The Hell Fire Club usually met in coffee houses like Daly's and Lucas' on Cork Hill near Dublin City Hall. The Lodge on Montpelier Hill in the Dublin Mountains was used as a hunting lodge. The membership consisted of rich young rakes that were into gambling, drinking, carousing and womanising.

Henry Lawes Luttrell, 2nd Earl of Carhampton (1743-1821), from a portrait by H.D. Hamilton, courtesy National Gallery of Ireland. Simon's son, Henry Lawes Luttrell, the 2nd Earl of Carhampton, was even more depraved than his father and grandfather. In company with Francis Higgins 'The Sham Squire' and others he procured an innocent 12-year-old girl called Mary Neill, who was brought to Mrs Llewlyn's establishment on the night of Carhampton's engagement party where she was ill used, as the records of the time coyly relate. The girl's parents arrived to rescue her but Carhampton, using his power, money and influence, tricked the authorities into believing that her parents had trafficked her. The unfortunate mother of the girl was imprisoned during the investigation and, while there, died in childbirth.

Carhampton walked away, free to continue on his life of debauchery. Mrs Llewlyn, the keeper of the wicked establishment, later became a tenant on the Luttrellstown estate, where she enjoyed Carhampton's protection. Local legends tell of a room in Luttrellstown Castle where a child was said to have died in suspicious circumstances.

Apart from his appalling personal life, Henry Luttrell, 2nd Earl of Carhampton, also did much to provoke the 1798 Rebellion. As Adjutant General of the Land Forces in Ireland he travelled around Westmeath, Leitrim, Longford and Roscommon with his 'Red Coats', press-ganging people into the British Navy and shipping them away. He was also notorious for pitch-capping suspected United Irishmen and burning their homes.

In 1797 James Dunne, a blacksmith and farmer on the Luttrellstown estate, along with another worker and tenant on the estate, Patrick Carty, and others in the United Irish Society, plotted to assassinate Carhampton but were betrayed by a man named Ferris. The two men were hanged from a tree near the bridge on the drive leading up to the castle, according to local sources.

Lord Carhampton was eventually relieved of his office as Commander of Land Forces by General Abercrombie, owing to his aggression to the civil populace in the 'mopping up' operations following the 1798 Rebellion. He did, however, continue to serve on the general staff of the British Army.

During the late 1700s and early 1800s Lord Carhampton was carrying out extensive refurbishment work on his Luttrellstown residence and much of the present castle's outward appearance and architecture dates back to that time.

It is believed that much of the work on the house may be the work of Sir Richard Morrison, who also designed Fota House, Kilruddery House and remodelled Shelton Abbey.

Luttrell sold the estate in 1811, having decamped to Painshill House in Surrey in 1807. He died there in 1821. The title passed to his brother John Olmious Luttrell as he had no children. When John Olmious Luttrell died in 1829 without any legitimate male heirs the title became extinct.

An illegitimate son of Henry Lawes Luttrell lived on until 1851. He was a society wit and poet and an associate of Lord Macaulay and Thomas Moore. He was Member of Parliament for Clonmines, County Wexford, in the last Irish parliament 1798.

An amusing story concerning Henry Lawes Luttrell's mortality is worth relating. The *Dublin Post* newspaper of 2 May 1811 reported the death of Henry Lawes Luttrell, 2nd Earl of Carhampton. Luttrell, being very much alive and incensed by the newspaper report, sent off a furious letter to the *Dublin Post*, demanding an immediate retraction. The next edition of the paper corrected their earlier death notice confirming that Luttrell was alive and well under the heading 'Public Disappointment'.

Mrs Anne Horton *née* Luttrell (1743-1808), painting by Thomas Gainsborough, courtesy National Gallery of Ireland. The Earl of Carhampton had three sisters, one, Lady Anne Luttrell, was born in 1743. Lady Anne, later the Duchess of Cumberland, had a reputation for using her undoubted beauty to her advantage and she was said to be liberal in the bestowing of her favours.

She was a stunning beauty noted for her most enchanting eyes. She was the widow of a Mr Christopher Horton when she became engaged to the Duke of Cumberland, brother of King George III. George III attempted to prevent the marriage owing to the lady's poor reputation but it went ahead in Calais. The King subsequently had Parliament enact a law prohibiting those in the royal succession from marrying without the permission of the monarch. The law is still in force.

Another sister, Lady Elizabeth, born in 1739, became a notorious gambler and was well known at the Faro tables. Faro was a particularly risky and exciting card game and was very popular with the nobility at the time, particularly with ladies. The Lady Elizabeth lost so much money that she was imprisoned for her debts and only got out of prison by marrying her hairdresser, thus transferring her debts to her unfortunate spouse. She was later arrested in Augsburg, Bavaria, as a pickpocket and was condemned to clean the streets of that city while chained to a wheelbarrow. The unfortunate lady died in prison by self-administered poison in 1797.

The remaining sister, Lady Lucy Luttrell, married Captain Joshua Moriarty, son of the Earl of Portarlington and led a less mercurial life than her siblings.

Luke White (c. 1740-1824), painting attributed to Stuart Gilbert (1755-1828). The new owner of Luttrellstown was Luke White, a native of the Isle of Man. He was a bookseller who achieved great wealth by his involvement with the lottery, but it was through selling tickets, not buying them. However, according to one story he stopped the Belfast coach and bought unsold tickets, believing that one of them was the winning ticket. He was correct and so fell into his fortune.

White was so wealthy that he loaned £500,000 to the Irish Exchequer in 1798 at 5 per cent.

He changed the name of the demesne from Luttrellstown to Woodlands owing to the widespread unpopularity of the Luttrell family name and continued the improvements to the castle and its surroundings.

Shortly after the sale of the property was agreed between White and Luttrell, and White had put down his deposit of £40,000, Luttrell discovered that White was not of noble birth and felt he was unworthy to own Luttrellstown. His snobbery surpassed his delight with the sale price of £180,000 and he demanded that White reverse the sale. White was more than a match for Luttrell and sent him off with a flea in his ear.

In 1818 Luke White became a Member of Parliament for Leitrim and served until his death in 1824. Henry White, Luke's son born in 1790, inherited the estate. He served in the British Army during the Peninsular War and was a Liberal Member of Parliament, first for Dublin and later for Longford.

Henry White, Lord Annaly, was raised to the peerage in 1863. He was a good landlord and supported local churches and schools and other communal interests.

Henry White was master of Luttrellstown in August 1849 when Queen Victoria, who was on an extended royal visit to Ireland, dropped in to Woodlands (as Luttrellstown was named at that time). She wore a distinctive green Irish poplin dress embroidered with gold shamrocks. Poplin was a blend of silk and fine wool and Dublin was famous for the production of this fabric. The Queen's visit coincided with a slump in the trade and it was hoped her choice of dress would give some impetus to this local industry.

Queen Victoria visited Ireland again in 1900 and took tea in the delightful glen on the estate. An obelisk of Wicklow granite stands there to commemorate the visit.

There is a local story that Henry White refused the local priest a site for the building of a school. The story goes that the National School in Porterstown, now unfortunately in a semi-ruinous state, was built high in an attempt to thwart him, it being visible from the castle windows. In fact the truth is that Henry White was generous to all faiths in the locality – Protestant and Catholic – and was a decent and good landlord.

He built, endowed and supported a school beside the then Catholic chapel in Porterstown. Unfortunately a dispute between Protestant and Catholic clergy concerning the management of the school occurred. Lord Annaly eventually put the school under the control of Fr Dungan, the parish priest of Blanchardstown.

Major Luke Henry White, 4th Baron Annaly (1885-1970), courtesy *Vanity Fair*. Major Luke Henry White married Lady Lavinia Spencer, the great-great-aunt of Princess Diana. Lavinia's mother, Margaret Baring, was a daughter of Lord Revelstoke of Barings Bank who was also the owner of Lambay Island.

Major Luke Henry White restored the name Luttrellstown to the demesne and sold it in 1915 to Maj. E.C. Hamilton. He then moved to Holdenby House in Northamptonshire.

During the First World War he was awarded the Legion of Honour and the Military Cross. He was a pilot officer in the Royal Air Force Reserve in the Second World War. He was also Justice of the Peace for Northamptonshire. He died in 1970.

Aileen Plunket, *née* Guinness, photographer unknown. Aileen Guinness lived at Luttrellstown Castle from 1930 until 1983, when she finally relocated to England.

Major Hamilton, the previous owner, died in 1918 and his widow sold it on to Arthur Ernest Guinness, brother of Lord Iveagh, who made a present of the house to his daughter Aileen as a wedding gift following her marriage to Brinsley Plunket in 1927.

They moved onto the 600-acre Luttrellstown estate in 1930. They had three daughters, Neelia, Doon and Maria; however, Maria died as a baby.

The Plunkets divorced in 1940 and Brinsley, who was an airman, was killed the following year while serving in the Royal Air Force. Aileen was devastated. She immersed herself in the running of the estate and her former employees say she was a good boss to work, for was approachable and had a good sense of humour. Local people living adjacent to the demesne have fond memories of her and I have personal memories of the wonderful garden fetes hosted by her in the castle grounds in aid of the local parish with the late comedian Jack Cruise acting as master of ceremonies.

Portrait of King Charles II, Luttrellstown Castle, painter unknown, photograph by author. In the 1950s Aileen Plunket engaged Felix Harbord, the noted interior decorator, to do a complete restoration and redecoration of the main rooms of the castle. He installed a large painting of an armour-clad King Charles II in the exclusive ermine robes of royalty over the grand marble fireplace in the staircase hall. To keep his majesty company Aileen Plunket hung portraits of some of his mistresses on the adjoining walls.

Aileen Plunket married Valerian Stux-Rybar, the design artist, in 1956 but they divorced in 1965 and she reverted to the name Plunket. Aileen's daughter Doon married the 5th Earl Granville, a cousin of Queen Elizabeth II, in 1958.

Aileen Plunket sold Luttrellstown in 1983 to the Primwest Group. She eventually moved to the United Kingdom after living for a while in Connemara. She died aged 94 in 1999.

Louise Kerouaille, Duchess of Portsmouth, painting unattributed. Louise Kerouaille's painting hangs in Luttrellstown Castle's Van Stry Room. She was reputed to be King Charles II's only true love. It was Louise who was with the King at his death and who ensured that he received the last rites of the Roman Catholic Church, according to his wishes.

Louise Kerouaille and King Charles have a very good reason to have their portraits displayed in Luttrellstown. They were, after all, the great-great-great-great-great-great-grandparents of Aileen Plunket through her maternal grandfather's line.

The King and Louise are also direct ancestors to – would you believe – the late Princess Diana, Sarah Ferguson and Camilla, Duchess of Cornwall.

The Entrance Hall, Luttrellstown Castle, photograph by author. The entrance hall is only a foretaste of the grandeur of Luttrellstown Castle. The Primwest Group bought Luttrellstown in 1983 and carried out lavish restoration work on the castle and its fourteen exquisitely furnished rooms. There are four reception rooms, a magnificent ballroom and facilities for swimming, tennis, fishing and shooting. There is also the opportunity of a round of golf on one of the finest championship courses in Ireland.

Visitors to Luttrellstown include President Regan, Prince Rainier and Princess Grace of Monaco, the Grand Duke of Luxembourg, the King and Queen of Denmark, Fred Astaire, Paul Newman, Douglas Fairbanks jnr, and recently Gerard Depardieu. Soccer star David Beckham and his wife Victoria Adams of Spice Girls fame tied the nuptial knot in Luttrellstown.

The castle changed hands again in 2006 and is now owned by a consortium consisting of J.P. McManus, John Magnier and Aidan Brooks.

Luttrellstown Boxing Club 1935/36, courtesy Nora Comiskey. This club was founded about 1935 and it's believed to have been formed at the instigation of the Hon. Brinsley Plunket of Luttrellstown Castle, who was a boxing enthusiast.

Identification of the boxers has been difficult given the passage of years. I have a copy of the programme for their first annual tournament in 1939. Boxers representing the Luttrellstown Club were M. Murray, J. Comiskey, P. McCafferty, M. Abbey, J. Geoghegan, G. Smith and H. Dignam. Some of these boxers may be in the photograph.

9

PHOENIX PARK

Dublin's Phoenix Park is only partly in the barony of Castleknock so I have excluded buildings and features that are outside the barony except where I could not resist the temptation, as was the case with the Wellington Monument.

The Viceregal Lodge, c. 1908, now Áras an Uachtaráin, courtesy Celia Burke, postcard picture unattributed. It looks very much like the work of Count Casimir Markievicz, husband of Constance Markievicz. He was working in Dublin around that period and paintings he did at that time have a similarity to this picture but without further research from an art expert it remains unattributed.

Before it became the Viceregal Lodge it was the Park Ranger's Lodge, built in 1751 by Nathaniel Clements, a kinsman of the Earls of Leitrim. Clements was descended from Daniel Clements, a Cromwellian soldier who was paid for his service in Cromwell's Model Army with land – the ancestral lands of the O'Reilly clan in Cavan – that had been forfeited.

The house was originally much smaller than it is now. It was described at the time it was built as a plain, brick building with offices projecting on each side connected by circular sweeps. It was in reality a hunting lodge, albeit a fine, well-constructed one. It has been greatly extended over the years and the design and workmanship is of the highest quality; it is a most beautiful building.

The position of park ranger was sinecure – a means of financially rewarding royal favourites. The real work of looking after the park was delegated to subordinates.

Nathaniel Clements died in 1777 and the government purchased the house five years later, for about £10,000, for use as a viceregal residence but it was only used occasionally. After the Act of Union (1801) it was decided to upgrade it to render it more suitable for the viceregal presence. The Lord Lieutenant, also known as the viceroy, represented the monarch of the day as the king or queen's deputy; indeed the post was called Lord Deputy in earlier times.

The first Viceroy Lord Lieutenant to move into Nathaniel Clement's house, by then retitled the Viceregal Lodge, was Fredrick Howard, 5th Earl of Carlisle. He was a cousin of Lord Byron and seemed to share a family trait for literary ability insofar as he wrote poems and plays, including two tragedies. Carlisle Bridge over the River Liffey, built in the years 1791 to 1794 ,was named after him. The bridge was reconstructed between 1877 and 1880 when the name was changed to O'Connell Bridge as the nearby O'Connell Monument was unveiled around that time.

The original hunting lodge was much improved and expanded on over the years. It is now a fine ninety-two-room mansion and, while it is not as large as some royal and presidential palaces elsewhere in the world, it is fit for purpose and has a dignity and beauty all of its own and a majestic parkland setting.

The Earl of Hardwick had the wings added in about 1803 and in 1808 the Duke of Richmond commissioned the fine Doric portico which was added to the north side. In 1816 the south portico with its Ionic columns was added by Francis Johnston (1760-1829), the architect who also designed the GPO and Nelson Pillar. The porticos are the work of Benjamin Henry Latrobe.

There were further extensions in 1849 for Queen Victoria's visit and again in 1911 for King George V's visit. Gas was connected in 1852 and electricity was installed in 1908.

The last viceroy, Lord Fitzalan, bade farewell to Ireland in 1922 and thus ended British rule in twenty-six of Ireland's thirty-two counties.

The new post of governor-general was given to Tim Healy, a member of the old Irish Parliamentary Party and Parnell's most vocal critic during the split in the Irish Party. When Ireland changed its constitution in 1937 Dr Douglas Hyde became the first President of Ireland the following year.

Áras an Uachtaráin is today the residence of the President of Ireland. The duties of the President include greeting distinguished visitors from other countries who come to our shores. Famous visitors to Áras an Uachtaráin include Pope John Paul II, Queen Elizabeth II and Prince Philip, Prince Charles, Emperor Akhito of Japan and his wife Empress Michiko, King Juan Carlos of Spain and his wife Queen Sophia, King Baudoin of Belgium, Prince Rainier III of Monaco and his wife Princess Grace, US Presidents John F. Kennedy, Richard Nixon, Ronald Reagan, Bill Clinton and Barrack Obama.

The gardens, lakes and grounds of the Viceregal Lodge, now Áras an Uachtaráin, are beautiful. The demesne of the Viceregal Lodge was originally 90 acres and additions over the years brought the size of the demesne up to 200 acres; however, 32 acres were ceded in recent times to Dublin Zoo for the African Plains Project. The design of the formal gardens is attributed to Decimus Burton whose influence is everywhere to be seen, not only in Áras an Uachtaráin but throughout the whole park. The landscape gardener Ninnian Niven, a native of Scotland, was very much involved in the laying out of the formal gardens.

The flower gardens in South Lawn were designed by Lady Normanby, wife of Lord Normanby, a very popular Lord Lieutenant. She was an accomplished gardener and was recognised as such by the professional gardeners in the Viceregal Lodge.

From 1852 until the 1890s George Smith from Perth in Scotland was head gardener and during his time it was said that he turned the Viceregal gardens into an efficient working school of horticulture.

All the demesnes in the park were reasonably self-sufficient. The Viceregal Lodge had venison from the Phoenix Park and before the advent of lawnmowers the sheep that grazed the lawns eventually graced the table accompanied by mint sauce. Fruit, vegetables and flowers were grown in the demesne. The orchards had pears, apples, cherries, and plums. There were glasshouses for peaches and pine stoves (glasshouses where pineapples were grown), vineries where the quality of the grapes was much commented on by guests. There were melon yards, asparagus beds, herb beds, kitchen gardens supplying carrots, onions, leeks, garlic, potatoes, turnips, celery, cabbage and lettuce plants, etc., and even mushroom houses.

The Under-Secretary's Lodge, later the Papal Nuncio's Residence, courtesy Office of Public Works. The former Under-Secretary's Lodge became the Papal Nuncio's residence in 1929. In 1975 the Nunciature in Phoenix Park was discovered to have a serious infestation of dry rot and the building had to be vacated. The Papal Nuncio transferred to a new building in the grounds of the Dominican convent in Cabra.

The former Nunciature was so badly infested it was decided to dismantle the building and in the process the building workers were amazed to discover that an old Irish tower house, that of Ashtown Castle, lay embedded in the late Georgian Ashtown Lodge. The old Irish tower house of Ashtown was first recorded in the Down Survey as follows:

> John Connell of Dublin Protestant Ashtowne one Plowland two Hundred acres, meadow 10 acres, arable 160 acres, pasture 23 acres, shrubwood 07. Valued by the Jury at seventy pounds. The proprietor helde the premises anno. 1641 as his inheritance. There is upon the premises one Castle with two Thatcht houses vallewed by the Jury at Eight Pounds. There is also one small orchard. The one moiety of the Tythes Belonged to the College (i.e Trinity) the other moiety to Sir Robert Meridith. [NB the spelling is as in the document of the time.]

John Connell of Ashtown Castle, an ancestor of Daniel O'Connell, exchanged his lands in Ashtown for Derrynane in County Kerry. There was a Daniel O'Connell who married an Alice Segrave of Cabragh and we know that Little Cabragh adjoined the lands of Pelletstown and Ashtown. He in turn had a son or grandson called John and we find a John Connell is living in Pelletstown at the time of the Restoration, in a house rated for four hearths. He also held lands at Ashtown, including one house rated as having three chimneys and believed to be the present castle.

The O'Connells seem to have previously given support to Queen Elizabeth I and are described as Protestant in the Down Survey. So, like many landowners and holders of office, they were trimming their religious sails to suit the prevailing wind. Note the absence of O' in the surname with some family members.

When James Butler, 12th Earl of Ormonde, was drawing together the lands we now know as Phoenix Park, he acquired the lands and castle of Ashtown in 1664.

The Phoenix Park was originally primarily a royal deer park for fallow deer, a breed introduced to Ireland by the Anglo-Normans in 1170. One of the deer keepers appointed by Viscount Dungannon was Sir William Flower who was assigned Ashtown Castle in 1668. He was followed by George Sackville and in 1785 Sackville Hamilton became Under-Secretary and he was given the post of keeper/ranger of Phoenix Park as well. In practice the job of keeper/ranger was delegated to a functionary who did the job for a fraction of what the Under-Secretary-cum-keeper/ranger was paid.

Several Under-Secretaries lived in Ashtown Lodge, as it had come to be called until the British left in 1922.

The castle or tower house seems to have been incorporated into the Georgian-style house in 1760. The magnificent walled gardens, where beautiful flowers, delicious vegetables and succulent fruits of every variety are grown, first appear on estate maps in 1853. These walled gardens are a must for visitors to Ashtown Castle – they are a classical example of the very best in Victorian kitchen garden design.

The gardener responsible for most of the work in designing the grounds was William Spalding Walker, who worked here from 1816 to 1832. He later became the park superintendent for the whole of Phoenix Park.

The Under-Secretary for Ireland was the permanent head of the British administration in Ireland, in other words, he ran the civil service. One of them was Thomas Drummond, who served from 1835 to 1840. He originally worked with the Ordnance Survey and was a brilliant engineer, mathematician and surveyor. He was a native of Scotland and when he became Under-Secretary he excelled at his job. He was followed by another former Ordnance Survey man, Thomas Larcom, who was also equally competent.

Thomas Henry Burke was assassinated while in office. He was killed along with Lord Cavendish by members of the Invincibles on 6 May 1882. He was in favour of Home Rule and reform of land issues but did not articulate these views because of his position as head of the civil service. However, he held office during the coercion acts that were introduced to halt Land League activity and because he was Irish and a Roman Catholic he was seen as a traitor by some.

The last Under-Secretary, Sir John Anderson, who served from 1920 to 1922, was known more for his later career in the British Cabinet. He was Lord Privy Seal in Chamberlain's government and advocated the development of a sheet metal cylinder made of pre-fabricated pieces that could be assembled and sunk in the garden of a house to act as an air-raid shelter during the Second World War. They were called Anderson shelters. During his time in Ireland he was eclipsed by his Assistant Under-Secretary Andy Cope who seemed to have a roving role as a go-between with Michael Collins, Eamon de Valera, James Craig and individual British Cabinet members in a kind of semi-official capacity that could be confirmed or denied as and when it suited either or both sides.

The Ashtown Lodge demesne became the residence for the United States legation in 1927 until they relocated to the former Chief Secretary's House in 1929. The Papal Nuncio occupied it from then until he moved to the new Nunciature in 1978.

The castle and its grounds are today a lively Visitors' Centre with an audiovisual display of the historical and environmental features of the park. There is also an excellent restaurant, the Fionn Uisce, which is noted for the quality of its food. The staff at the Visitors' Centre are very knowledgeable, have a keen sense of history and are helpful and friendly.

Ashtown Castle, an Irish tower house hidden within the structure of the Georgian-style Under-Secretary's Lodge, photograph by Andrew Lacey.

Ashtown Castle – The Walled Garden, photograph by Andrew Lacey. The Walled Garden in Ashtown Castle appears on estate maps for the first time in 1853. The Walled Garden, however, evolved from the kitchen garden and may have been laid out some years earlier. The garden is probably the design of William Spalding Walker (1794-1870) who was employed in Ashtown Castle demesne before eventually becoming superintendent of Phoenix Park. This walled garden is an example of Victorian garden design at the peak of its perfection.

THE CHIEF SECRETARY'S LODGE.

The Chief Secretary's Lodge, now Deerfield, the residence of the Ambassador of the United States of America, courtesy Office of Public Works.

The Chief Secretary was the political head of the British administration in Ireland; the Under-Secretary made most of the day-to-day decisions relating to the government of Ireland and was effectively head of the Civil Service; and the Lord Lieutenant or Viceroy lived nearby in the Viceregal Lodge (now Áras an Uachtaráin) and he was the representative of the British monarchy in Ireland. Thus Phoenix Park was home to this triumvirate that ruled Ireland.

The warren of offices that existed in and around Dublin Castle were the engine that drove British rule in Ireland but the tiller that steered it was firmly in Phoenix Park, albeit with three hands on the tiller at times.

The Chief Secretary's Lodge in Phoenix Park was originally a modest four-bedroomed Bailiff's Lodge and was acquired by Sir John Blacquire who was appointed Park Bailiff in 1774. He had previously been appointed as Chief Secretary for Ireland in 1772. The house was greatly enlarged by Blacquire and was home to successive Chief Secretaries until 1922, when the final departure of the British administration from Ireland took place.

The Chief Secretary's Lodge remained vacant until 1927 when the United States appointed Fredrick Sterling as its envoy to the Irish Free State. The United States took out a 999-year lease on the property at that time and used it both as the chancellery and the residence. It is now used exclusively as the residence of the United States ambassador. The chancellery is in Ballsbridge.

Sir John Blacquire turned the demesne into what it is today. He was the son of French Huguenots who arrived in England in 1685, having escaped religious persecution in their native county. Sir John Blacquire was born in 1732 and joined the British Army, rising up the ranks to become a lieutenant colonel. He was appointed as Secretary of Legation in the British Embassy in Paris, probably because of his family origins in France and an ability to converse easily in the French language. There he reported to Lord Harcourt, the British ambassador, and they became firm friends. So it was no surprise when Harcourt was promoted to Lord Lieutenant and Viceroy of Ireland in 1772 that Blacquire accompanied him here as Chief Secretary.

Harcourt had pursued a successful military career and raised a regiment the 76th Foot (Lord Harcourt's Regiment) to help put down Bonnie Prince Charlie's Jacobite Rebellion in 1745. While Chief Secretary in Ireland he proposed a 10 per cent tax on absentee landlords and adopted a conciliatory position in Ireland, persuading Henry Flood to accept government office. He died while trying to rescue his dog from a well in 1777.

Sir John Blacquire was involved in founding the Catholic Committee along with eminent Catholics such as Lord Kenmare and Lord Trimblestown. This committee did much to bring about the gradual repeal of the Penal Laws.

Two years into his office of Chief Secretary John Blacquire was appointed Park Bailiff and occupied the Bailiff's house on 35 acres of land. He greatly enlarged the house and acquired another 27 acres of land to bring the size of the demesne up to 62 acres, the second largest demesne in the park after the Viceregal Lodge.

Blacquire was later given unlimited grazing rights in the park for his cattle and sheep. A spirited ballad was written at the time about this, dubbing Blacquire as the king's cowboy. The nickname stuck.

Having acquired the house from the government as Park Bailiff he sold it back to them in 1782 for use as a residence for his successor, the incoming Chief Secretary, for £7,000. Sir John's salary for the job of Bailiff had risen to £500 per annum; however, he appointed a Deputy Bailiff to do the job for him for £55 2s 6d per year.

Arthur Wellesley, later to become Duke of Wellington and Prime Minister, served as Chief Secretary in 1807 and 1808.

Robert Peel was Chief Secretary from 1812 to 1818. While living in the Phoenix Park he proposed the setting up of a modern, specialised police force. The nickname 'bobby' for London policemen comes from Peel's first name Robert as he founded the London Metropolitan Police. In Ireland they used his second name to create the more pejorative sounding 'peeler' for a policeman. O'Connell gave him the nickname 'orange Peel' because of his opposition to Catholic emancipation. He served as Prime Minister twice. His son, Robert Peel, was also Irish Chief Secretary from 1861 to 1865.

Lord Frederick Cavendish did not last long in the post; in May 1882 he was assassinated by the Invincibles a couple of hundred yards from the gates of the Chief Secretary's demesne on the day he took his oath as Chief Secretary.

Another Chief Secretary was W.H. Smith, the famous bookseller. When he took up the job in 1886 he turned over his Dublin branch to his manager Charles Eason. However, within four days the government resigned and Smith's job was gone. He went back to selling books and Charles Eason continued running his business. To this day both W.H. Smith's and Easons are still in business.

The last Chief Secretary to live here was Sir Hamar Greenwood, who was born in Canada and who will always be remembered for his support for the Black and Tans and the Auxiliaries during the War of Independence. In denying the policy of reprisals he is purported to have said, 'There are no such thing as reprisals but they have done a great deal of good.' He departed from Dublin in 1922 unwept, unhonoured and unsung.

The United States took over the former Chief Secretary's House and demesne in 1927. The entrance gates, with a central arch for vehicular traffic flanked on each side by matching arched pedestrian gates and further flanked by matching gate lodges, are particularly beautiful. The entrance is believed to be the work of Jacob Owen and the inscribed gates were designed by Richard Turner, who also designed the magnificent glasshouses in the Botanic Gardens, Glasnevin.

Ivor Guest, 1st Viscount Wimborne, was Lord Lieutenant during the 1916 Rising and was a first cousin of Winston Churchill. Ironically Wimborne's nephew, Raymond Guest, was United States Ambassador to Ireland during the fiftieth anniversary celebrations of the Easter Rising. When Guest was presenting his credentials to President de Valera in Áras an Uachtaráin, de Valera jokingly said to him, 'You must be familiar with this place', in a reference to Guest's uncle's residency. Guest replied, 'Sir, like your distinguished self, I was born in New York.'

Another American Ambassador who served here was Jean Kennedy-Smith, sister of the late President John Fitzgerald Kennedy. She lived there during the 1990s.

In June 1963 I was one of a group of kids that cycled up to the United States Ambassador's residence to see if we could get a glimpse of President Kennedy. We had just arrived at the gates when his limo and convoy swept up to the gates. He instructed his driver to stop and leant out and shook as many of our hands as he could until anxious security men urged him to move on.

Little Lodge, Phoenix Park, photographer unknown. The Churchill family, in fact three generations of the family, arrived in Dublin at the end of 1876. Lord Randolph Churchill, his wife the former Jenny Jerome, and their son Winston and they came to live in the Little Lodge at the rear of Áras an Uachtaráin. Grandad, the 7th Duke of Marlborough, had just been ensconced in the main house the vice regal lodge, today's Áras an Uachtaráin, home of the President of Ireland.

The Little Lodge is today known as Ratra House and is used by the Civil Defence Corps. It was occupied by our first President, Dr Douglas Hyde, on his retirement from office in 1945 until his death in 1949. Ratra was the name of Dr Hyde's former home in County Roscommon.

The arrival of the Churchills coincided with the appointment of John Winston Churchill, 7th Duke of Marlborough as Lord Lieutenant of Ireland. Lord Randolph was his son and was there to act as his father's private secretary. The 'promotion' of the Duke of Marlborough had its origin in a scandal involving Edward, Prince of Wales.

Randolph had information concerning the Prince which he threatened to use if a divorce case, in which his brother Blanford was named as co-respondent, was not dropped. Prime Minister Disraeli, in response on Queen Victoria's authority, offered Marlborough the Lord Lieutenancy on the basis that he and his family would be of greater service to the Crown by increasing their distance from court. The job offer could not be refused and, to the delight of the Exchequer the position involved an outlay of non-refundable expenses of £40,000 per annum for a salary of £20,000 per annum.

Lord Randolph would not have been unfamiliar with his brother's difficulties as he too had a liberal attitude in matters of marital fidelity. His wife Jenny Jerome, daughter of New York financier Leonard W. Jerome, was a woman of stunning and exotic beauty. She was reputed to be of Iroquois descent and her good looks were said to reflect these roots. Her Native American bloodline was often mentioned by Winston Churchill, particularly on his travels in the USA and Canada. While living in Dublin Jenny gave birth to another son, John Strange Churchill.

It has been said that Jenny had over 200 lovers, including the Prince of Wales, who was associated with her briefly prior to her marriage to Lord Randolph. Following Randolph's death she renewed her friendship with the Prince, or 'Tum-Tum', as she affectionately called him. When Edward fell for Alice Kepple, Jenny married George Cornwallis West, a young officer in the Scots Guards in 1890. He was at least twenty years younger than her and only sixteen days older than Winston. They divorced in 1914.

She married again in 1918 to a much younger man – he was three years younger than Winston. His name was Montague Phippen Porch. Jenny died from a haemorrhage following a fall down a staircase in June 1921.

Winston was a lonely child, spending hours on end deploying little tin soldiers in various military formations. He had little contact with either parent, not uncommon in upper-class families at that time. Churchill spoke later on in life that his first memory was of his grandfather, the Duke of Marlborough, unveiling the statue of Lord Gough in Phoenix Park. Churchill outlived the statue, which was blown up in 1957 by an 'illegal organisation' as the newspapers of the day quaintly described it when a three-letter acronym would have sufficed.

The lack of parental affection that Winston Churchill suffered was more than redeemed by the devotion of his nanny, Mrs Elizabeth Everest. In his memoirs he tells of an incident that occurred while riding his little donkey, accompanied by his nanny through the park. She spotted a military group marching intently towards them. She thought them to be Fenians because of their dark green uniforms. She took to her heels with great alacrity with the unfortunate Winston and donkey in tow. In the ensuing pandemonium Winston was thrown by the donkey, landed on his head and suffered slight concussion. The uniforms were actually the bottle green ones of the Royal Irish Constabulary on parade from the nearby depot. Churchill cited this event as his first introduction to Irish politics and a painful one at that.

A more sombre memory was receiving the present of a drum from a Mr Burke. Some years later, when back in England, he learned of the assassination of the same Mr Burke and Lord Cavendish in Phoenix Park. He also remembered witnessing a great fire that destroyed the old Theatre Royal in Hawkins Street in 1880.

During the War of Independence, as British rule in Ireland became unworkable, Churchill proposed a solution based on his premise 'Get three generals if you cannot get three judges' and imposed the Black and Tans and the Auxiliaries on Ireland. During these years he would take no criticism of these forces and defended their actions in spite of overwhelming evidence of atrocities. Yet when the chance came for a truce in 1921 he, more than any other member of Cabinet, spoke forcefully in favour of it. King George V let it be known that he was personally shocked and embarrassed at the behaviour of the Crown forces in Ireland and this may have altered Churchill's position.

When the treaty negotiations were going on Churchill was very firm, gave little or nothing and pushed very hard, endorsing Lloyd George's threat 'of immediate and terrible war'. Although aloof at first during the negotiations, he had some banter with Michael Collins. Collins at one stage remonstrated with Churchill as to how the British had hunted him down, night and day, and even put a price on his head. In reply, Churchill showed Collins a similar proclamation the Boers had posted about himself in 1899 and Collins burst out laughing and the atmosphere thawed.

Students of history and politics have for years debated as to whether or not Churchill was a friend to Ireland. The issue probably never entered Churchill's mind. His sole concern was Britain and her empire, and every other nation's welfare was incidental. To him the freedom of Ireland was a gift bestowed by imperial benevolence and not a right to nationhood by entitlement and the nature of the gift was a loan. He said as much in his infamous speech at the close of the Second World War when he praised 'the restraint and poise' exercised by the British Government in relation to neutral Ireland. '[We] never laid a violent hand upon them even though at times it would have been quite easy and natural.' Eamon de Valera replied: 'Mr Churchill makes it clear that in certain circumstances he would have violated our neutrality and that he would justify his action by Britain's necessity – if accepted, it would mean that Britain's necessity would become a moral code and when this necessity became sufficiently great other people's rights, were not to count ....' De Valera had hit the nail on the head. It was Churchill's moral code and not only that of Churchill but that of the whole ruling class of Britain. It was the essence of empire.

When Churchill died in January 1965 his funeral was attended by ten heads of state and representatives of 112 countries, including former IRA Chief of Staff Frank Aiken who was then Minister of External Affairs for the Republic of Ireland.

Incidentally, Churchill's ghost, in the form of a child, has reportedly been seen in Áras an Uachtaráin, the former Vice Regal Lodge where his grandfather the Duke of Marlborough once held court.

The Little Lodge, courtesy Office of Public Works, Phoenix Park. The Little Lodge was the residence of the private secretary to the Viceroy.

The Duke of Marlborough, Lord Lieutenant of Ireland, unveils the Gough Memorial in Phoenix Park, from *The Graphic*, 13 March 1880. On 22 July 1957 the fine equestrian statute was blown up by, as the papers of the day described, an 'illegal organisation'.

There is a story, which may be apocryphal, that earlier that day the Taoiseach Mr de Valera was the recipient of a telegram advising him that a horse would be running in the park and he should be on it. The cryptic message could be construed as a tip for a horse as the Phoenix Park racecourse was usually referred to as 'the Park'. The Taoiseach and his advisors were puzzled. It was not until the following morning when the statue of Gough sitting astride his horse was lying in pieces across the main road of the park that the Taoiseach realised the import of the message and he was not amused. The mischievous message was supposedly the work of the late Brendan Behan, who was known to be sympathetic to the organisation responsible for the explosion.

Dr Douglas Hyde, Ireland's first President, photographer unknown. The new Constitution of 1937 removed the position of Governor General and required an elected President so Taoiseach Eamon de Valera met with W.T. Cosgrave, then leader of the opposition. They agreed that they needed someone of character and prestige and yet someone who might not be too headstrong or authoritarian – in the Europe of the time there were quite enough authoritarian dictators. They also felt that it would be better to have a person of another religion than Roman Catholic as they wanted to disprove the assertion that the State was a 'confessional state'.

Both admired Dr Douglas Hyde, a university professor who was fluent in French, German, Greek, Latin and Hebrew. He was an Irish-language activist and was a founder of Conradh na Gaeilge. He was the son of a Church of Ireland rector and so fitted the bill perfectly. President Hyde was inaugurated as the first President of Ireland on 26 June 1938. A feature of the ceremony was that the President's Declaration of Office was in his native Roscommon dialect of Irish – the recording made at this ceremony is the last recording ever made in Ireland of that now disappeared dialect.

The President did not enjoy good health and died on 12 July 1949. Roman Catholic rules at the time did not allow its members to attend the services of other religious denominations. All of the Cabinet adhered to this ruling with the exception of Noël Browne. Eamon de Valera did not risk attending either and sent Erskine Childers, a Church of Ireland member of the party, along to represent him. So much for Ireland not being a 'confessional state'.

The Little Lodge as it is now, photograph by author. The Little Lodge was structurally altered and renamed Ratra House when it became Dr Douglas Hyde's home on his retirement from the presidency. It was used from then as headquarters of the Civil Defence until four years ago, when An Gaisce, the President's Awards Scheme, moved into offices there.

Lord Frederick Cavendish and Thomas H. Burke were assassinated in Phoenix Park in May 1882, photographer unknown. On a Saturday evening, 6 May 1882, Under-Secretary Thomas Burke and the newly appointed Chief Secretary, Lord Frederick Cavendish, were assassinated on the main road, Chesterfield Road, Phoenix Park.

Earlier that evening the inauguration ceremonies had been held in Dublin Castle for the succession of John Poyntz Spencer, 5th Earl Spencer KG to the Lord Lieutenancy of Ireland. (Diana, Princess of Wales, was to bring greater fame to the Spencer Family.) Lord Frederick Charles Cavendish and Thomas H. Burke Under-Secretary were in attendance and on the conclusion of the formalities they set off separately for the Viceregal Lodge (now Áras an

Uachtaráin). Cavendish left on foot shortly after 7 p.m., followed some while later by Burke travelling by cab. Burke caught up with Cavendish at Park Gate Street and dispensed with his cab, continuing on foot with his companion in the direction of the Vice Regal Lodge.

Within 300 yards of the Phoenix Column the two men were attacked by men wielding 12-inch long surgical knives. Burke was identified by a Dublin Castle employee named Joe Smith. Initially, Joe Brady knelt down in their path, pretending to tie his bootlaces in a ruse to slow their progress. Brady lunged at Burke, knifing him in the back. Tim Kelly went for Cavendish, stabbing him repeatedly while Cavendish tried to fight him off while shouting for help from passers-by. Brady cut Burke's throat and Brady, Kelly, Caffrey and Delaney were whisked away in a cab driven by Michael Kavanagh. He would later give evidence against them. The others, Curley, Fagan and Hanlo,n fled the scene in a cab driven by James 'skin the goat' Fitzharris.

Burke died almost immediately and Cavendish was breathing his last breath when two cyclists came on the scene to lend assistance. Most onlookers thought it was a drunken brawl, as did one of Earl Spencer's officers who witnessed the scene from the windows of the Vice Regal Lodge.

A cab had been seen exiting through Chapelizod gate at great speed. That was all the police had to go on. The assailants belonged to 'The Invincibles'. They were a splinter group of the Fenian movement. They were seeking independence for Ireland and were also involved in disputes connected with landlord and tenant issues. Many tenant farmers were paying rack rents and if they made improvements to the land the landlord increased their rent. Tenure of land was at the discretion of the landlord and he could remove them at will. The land agitation and the desire for independence were supported by many and even moderate requests for Home Rule met with government rejection. The Invincibles appealed to those who had lost patience with the government and their own more moderate leaders.

The men involved, most of them from humble backgrounds, were acting on the instructions of James Carey their leader. Unlike the others he was reasonably 'well to do', a builder, landlord and town councillor.

The political fallout was immediate, causing immense embarrassment to the Land League, Parnell and the Irish Party in Westminster. Cavendish was married to Prime Minister Gladstone's niece Lucy and had been appointed by Gladstone as a goodwill emissary to Ireland. Strangely enough the Invincibles did not realise that Burke's companion was Lord Cavendish. Their target was Burke because he was Irish-born and a Roman Catholic, and was, therefore, in their eyes, a betrayer of his country and religion.

Eight months later Superintendent Mallon of the Dublin Metropolitan Police had rounded them all up. Mallon tricked the Dublin leader of the Invincibles, Carey, into informing by leading him to believe that he was being betrayed. The following were executed: Joe Brady, Michael Fagan, Daniel Curley, Thomas Caffrey and Tim Kelly. The hangings were carried out by William Marwood in Kilmainham Gaol. Marwood was paid a retainer of £20 per annum plus £10 for each execution. There was an added bonus whereby the hangman was allowed to keep the deceased's garments. They were usually sold to Madame Tussaud's gallery.

There was little public sympathy for the Invincibles. The killings were messy – knives were never a weapon of first choice for physical force republicans – and the victims were both unarmed. The events mired the Land League's and Parnell's efforts in the Irish Party and caused anti-Irish rioting in England.

On the other hand, there was no time for Carey and other informers and to this day a 'carey' is Dublin slang for a spy or a traitor.

The scene outside the Viceregal's Lodge following the assassinations of Thomas H. Burke and Lord Henry Cavendish, picture from *Illustrated London News*, May 1882.

The author's great-aunt was called as a witness at the trials. She lived in the gate lodge of the Under-Secretary's and one of the Invincibles, possibly Joe Brady, had called the previous day enquiring as to Mr Burke's movements. The cross-examination was very rigorous as she was unable to identify the caller and she never fully recovered from the ordeal.

Phoenix Park School in 1998, painting by Mary McMenamin. This was formerly a National School, built in 1847/48 to cater for the children of the many Phoenix Park employees whose homes were within the confines of the park. It catered for local children from Blackhorse Lane and Ashtown as well. It is now the Phoenix Park Special School and caters for children with emotional and behavioural difficulties. The school appears regularly on TV during election time as it is used as a polling station and it's where the President casts his or her vote.

A fine day near the Wellington Monument, photographer unknown. The Wellington Monument, designed by Sir Robert Smirke RA, was at one time the tallest obelisk in the world at 205ft. The tallest obelisk in the world today is the 555ft Washington Monument, completed in 1884. The Wellington Monument was started in 1817, only two years after the Battle of Waterloo, but was not finished until 1861, nine years after his death. It was originally planned for St Stephen's Green and after much debate was placed in its present location. The area was formerly used as a saluting battery where cannons roared out a welcome to important visitors.

The obelisk was officially called the Wellington Testimonial but it was changed to the Wellington Monument; however, cheeky 'Dubs' called it the Overgrown Milestone. To generations of Dublin kiddies it was known as 'The Slippery Steps' owing to the difficulty in scaling the eleven steeply sloping steps and the great difficulty in coming back down. The railway line linking Heuston and Connolly railway stations runs under the park, very close to the monument.

There is an old canard that Wellington disowned his Dublin birth saying, 'If he was born in a stable it would not make him a horse'. It was actually Daniel O'Connell who said it of Wellington. Wellington was quite proud of his Dublin birth and he was kind to Ireland, bringing Catholic emancipation into law in 1929.

Mountjoy Barracks, Phoenix Park, c. 1820, painting by Samuel Frederick Brocas (1792-1847), courtesy National Library of Ireland. Mountjoy House was originally a private house but later the house and its demesne became a cavalry barracks and parade ground for the Castleknock Cavalry and is today the Ordnance Survey offices.

The house was home to Luke Gardiner, the famous property developer and politician. Luke Gardiner, his son Charles and his grandson Luke reshaped the face of Dublin, laying out the fine squares, wide streets and majestic buildings that are a particular feature of Georgian Dublin. Indeed, their work continues to beautify our city and assists our exchequer by attracting visitors here from all over the world who come to view the finest examples of Georgian architecture anywhere in the world.

The Gardiner family were good employers and did not discriminate on religious grounds; politically they supported the government but urged for a relaxation of the Penal Laws that discriminated against Catholics and dissenting Protestants. They gave their family name to Gardiner Street and their noble title, Mountjoy, to Mountjoy Square and Mountjoy Prison. Incidentally, of Dublin's five Georgian Squares the only one that is a true square is Mountjoy Square; each side is exactly 140 metres long. The square was built between 1790 and 1818 and Arthur Guinness was one of its first residents. He died there in 1804.

The first Luke Gardiner was a park keeper. In those days a park keeper was a highly paid position – Luke wasn't going around clipping hedges, sweeping pathways and picking up litter, but he made sure that others did. His area of responsibility was the Castleknock end of the park. He built a private house on 16 acres in that end of the park in 1728. It did not become to be known as Mountjoy House until his grandson, another Luke Gardiner, was raised to the peerage as Lord Mountjoy. Many of the stones used to build the house were the recycled rubble of the remains of Tyrrell's Castle of Castleknock, then in the ownership of the Warren family of Corduff. In fact, Mountjoy House was built on land that was sold to the Phoenix Park by the Warrens.

Luke Gardiner's grandson, Lord Mountjoy, was a member of the Irish Volunteers and raised a troop of cavalry for the volunteers known as the Castleknock Cavalry. Lord Mounjoy was a moderate and deplored Adjutant General Henry Lawes Luttrell's policy of coercion and only joined the government forces in putting down the rebellion when pressed. He died at the Battle of New Ross in 1798 while fighting on the government side against the Wexford insurgents. It is said that he was killed while attempting to parley with the rebels in an effort to avoid further bloodshed.

Luke Gardiner was fascinated with the theatre so much so that he had a theatre built at Mountjoy House and he staged many plays, including most of William Shakespeare's many works.

In 1922 the Ordnance Survey became an element of the Irish Army and remained so until the 1970s when it started to introduce civilian staff. Today almost all of the Survey's mapping is by aerial photography and on almost every day of the year the two Ordnance Survey aircraft are crossing back and forth over the State, mapping and measuring. The Ordnance Survey provides the Central Statistics Office and other government departments with high-quality maps. Ongoing work is being carried out amalgamating geographical co-ordinates with postal codes for every address in the State to ensure better and more accurate mail delivery and other essential services. The Ordnance Survey currently has 320 staff located in Phoenix Park and in six regional offices.

10

CHAPELIZOD

Chapelizod, County Dublin, in the late 1890s, Lawrence Collection, courtesy National Library of Ireland. Chapelizod was once a walled town with a large military barracks, a thriving linen industry and the home of many figures who would achieve fame in the world of literature. The Lord Deputy or Irish Viceroy's official State residence was on the site of what is now the Chapelizod industrial estate. William of Orange stayed there for a while after the Battle of the Boyne. Henry John Temple, 3rd Viscount Palmerston, who was British Prime Minister for two terms in 1855-1858 and again from 1859-1865, was a member of the Temple family who were once landlords of Chapelizod and Palmerstown.

The Temple family sold their lands to Robert Wilcox from Mountmellick. He in turn sold them in 1763 to John Hely Hutchinson.

Chapelizod was on the Phoenix Park side of the River Liffey and in the Barony of Castleknock. The opposite side was known as St Laurence after a house built for the accommodation of people suffering from leprosy. St Laurence has been in the Barony of Uppercross since 1898 and before that it was in the Barony of Newcastle. At that time the disease was often misdiagnosed and people suffering from other skin diseases and blemishes found themselves in leper houses. The leper house was dissolved early in the fourteenth century as the disease had faded away in Ireland. It is believed that this terrible disease was originally brought back from the Middle East by infected pilgrims returning from the Holy Land.

This side of the river was also known as Teach Guaire or Stagori. Guaire was a king of Connacht in the seventh century and he may have had some connection with the locality. Chapelizod was a walled town and it had a mill and a weir and a salmon fishery during the early thirteenth century. We know the name comes from the Norman French *Chapelle Iseult*, meaning Iseult's Chapel. The name first appears in records in the year 1220 in Latin as *Capella Isolda*. It may have got its name from the legendary story of Tristan from Cornwall and Isolda, an Irish princess, who fell in love. They were forcibly parted but when they eventually died they were buried in adjoining graves. A tree grew out of each plot and the branches of the two trees grew entwined each other – so the lovers were eventually joined.

There was an Isolda's Tower in the walls of Dublin city and an Isolda's Well between Kilmainham and Chapelizod so the name was in use at that time.

The Down Survey records it as Chappelizzard. It's called simply The Lizard by most locals. The De La Felde family, who lived in the area for years, owned part of Chapelizod as well as lands in Corduff. Sir Henry Power Lord Valentia, an Elizabethan adventurer, was granted the manor of Chapelizod for services to the Crown. He served with the Earl of Essex in Munster and sailed with Sir Francis Drake.

Lord Valentia built a large house in what is today's industrial estate. The house was an imposing structure with fifteen chimneys. William of Orange stayed here for a while after the Battle of the Boyne as it was the then viceregal residence. Due to his short stay there it became known as the King's House.

Sir Richard Lawrence set up a new industry for the manufacture of linen and other textiles, including woollen goods in or about 1670. He brought in French Huguenot workers experienced in linen manufacture from La Rochelle and the Ile de Ré to man the factory.

The Lovett family then took over the business. Christopher Lovett became Lord Mayor of Dublin. His wife was a direct descendent of Rory O'Moore and her sister married John Knox, the Scottish religious reformer. Lovett's grandson, Edward Lovett Pearce, was one of several architects involved in the design of the magnificent Houses of Parliament, now the Bank of Ireland in College Green.

The woollen business at this time suffered a steep decline owing to government interference. The government was more interested in building up English woollen exports.

The Crosthwaite family then took over the linen mill and it thrived. Several hundred people worked in the mill. The Crosthwaites were good employers and they assisted financially in the education of local children and were generous with local churches, both Catholic and Protestant. William Dargan (of railway fame) opened a nearby mill for spinning thread from locally grown flax and the thread achieved a top award at the Paris Exhibition of 1855.

Phoenix Park Distillery, Chapelizod, early 1900s, drawing unattributed. The site was originally occupied by a linen mill but for various reasons, mainly mechanisation and better organisation of the workforce, the growing of flax and the spinning of linen relocated to the north of Ireland and the factory and mill were sold to Scottish distillers.

Chapelizod's Spinning Mill became a distillery in 1878. The rebuild and conversion of the premises cost between £30,000 and £40,000 at the time and was carried out by the Distillers Company Ltd, a Scottish company. The architect contracted to carry out the conversion, Edward Henry Carson, was Lord Edward Carson's father. The Carson family were originally from Dumfriesshire in Scotland.

At that time the company prospectus stated 'the demand for Irish whiskey is practically unlimited at present'. There were over 100 whisky distillers in Scotland, whereas in Ireland there were only twenty. The demand for Irish whiskey was five times that of Scotch. The quality and reputation of Dublin-made whiskey was greater than whiskey distilled elsewhere in Ireland and secured a much better price.

The Chapelizod Company took its name from the nearby Phoenix Park and selected an image of the Phoenix Monument as their trademark, trading as the Phoenix Park Distillery.

Despite being the smallest of all distilleries owned by the Distillers Company Ltd, it was its most modern and efficient one. The power used in the distillery was water power from the Liffey and the waterwheel extracting the power from the river Liffey was 70ft in breadth and

18ft in diameter and was the largest waterwheel in the British Isles at that time. The wheel even generated the electricity from an Elwell-Parker dynamo that powered the incandescent lamps for the factory.

The distillery covered 6 acres. There were four pot stills in the still house, containing 36,000 gallons of whiskey between them. There were 16,000 casks of maturing whiskey in 6 bonded warehouses. The site included a racking store, a cooperage, a blacksmiths and carpentry works. The houses in New Row were built for workers who came over from Scotland to work in the distillery and those houses are still there to this day.

In 1886 sixty men were employed there and 350,000 gallons of whiskey were produced each year. The firm closed following independence in 1923 as one of its biggest clients, the British War Office, decided to keep its business within the United Kingdom.

The Mullingar House Chapelizod, the setting for James Joyce's *Finnegans Wake*, photographer unknown. The Mullingar House is so called because it's on the road to Mullingar. It was one of the many taverns that existed in Chapelizod where there was a large army barracks and some industry guaranteeing plenty of thirsty customers.

11

STRAWBERRY BEDS

The Strawberry Beds is without doubt the most beautiful area of the Barony of Castleknock. The area was, and still is to a certain extent, dotted with cosy homesteads, each with their own pretty garden. Strawberries were grown here for a couple of hundred years, giving the area its name; however, the south-facing slopes grew more than strawberries. It was a great area for all sorts of vegetables and flowers, including peas, cabbages and onions. The sloping ground that captured every ray of sun meant plants had to be regularly watered. This was not an easy task as water had to be hauled from wells or the river up steep slopes.

Strawberries are not in fact berries at all but an aggregate accessory fruit. The strawberries we eat today are a hybrid species descended from a cross between strawberries from North America, *Fragaria virginiana*, and strawberries from Chile, *Fragaria chiloenses*. The Chilean strawberry was first brought to France in 1714. The cross between the two varieties was first bred in Brittany in the 1750s. Prior to this, wild strawberries *Fragaria sylvestris* were gathered in the forests, where we can still find them today. They are much smaller but sweeter than the cultivated ones.

In May 1791 a French diplomat, Charles Coquebert, passed through this area and described the slopes of the Liffey valley as being covered with strawberry plants, peas, cabbage, etc., and speculates that the south-facing slopes might be suitable for growing grapevines. He also mentions that the inhabitants of Dublin came here on pleasure trips.

Dr Marmaduke Coghill of Leixlip and 'All Hallows' House, Drumcondra (now a Vincentian college), imported Chilean strawberries from France in 1740 and cultivated them in his Leixlip estate. So by the time of Coqueberts's visit the cultivation of strawberry plants had extended to here at Strawberry Beds.

To this day it is a very special place inhabited by very special people who give a great welcome to visitors. The local hostelries are very popular with live music and entertainment at weekends and sometimes during the week.

Strollers enjoying the Strawberry Beds near the Anglers' Rest, courtesy Fingal County Council. This pub, at the Dublin end of the Strawberry Beds, is now owned by Wrights of Howth and has a fine seafood restaurant. It dates back at least to the early 1800s and was a hotel where anglers stayed while fishing the great salmon fishery of the Liffey River. The salmon have returned but fishing is restricted at present.

In the summers of the 1800s and early 1900s Dubliners would come in their droves to eat the strawberries and cream served up on a fresh clean cabbage leaf. The daintier establishments served the fruit and cream on a lettuce leaf – either way, it was organic packaging with no washing up!

Strawberry Hall in the early 1900s, courtesy Declan Cummins, Strawberry Hall. Strawberry Hall is famous for its great pint; it is also a picture gallery and a museum. Over the years Declan Cummins, the proprietor, has amassed a great selection of photographs and prints relating to Irish history. He has a fantastic collection of memorabilia such as police equipment dating back to the early 1800s, including helmets and buckles and truncheons. There are also musical instruments, old tools and kitchen equipment.

Mrs Williams, who owned the establishment, catered for off-duty members of the Royal Irish Constabulary who would cycle out from the city or from their depot in Phoenix Park. The surrounding hills and dales of the Strawberry Beds made for hard pedalling that drove the thirsty cyclists straight to her door. Mrs Williams was a loyal supporter of the British Empire so the constables relaxed in comfort.

Today the Strawberry Hall still caters for people who also prefer to journey on two wheels but without the pedalling. Motorcyclists take a spin out most weekends for a chat with others of the motorcycling fraternity or to have a game of bar billiards. The Strawberry Hall is one of fewer than half a dozen pubs around Dublin that still has a table for this exciting game.

Strawberry Hall today, photograph by author. There used to be a great festival in the Strawberry Beds in July with all sorts of stalls and sports, pubs with sing-songs and the Blanchardstown Brass Band playing in the festival field and, of course, strawberries and cream. It lapsed in the 1980s owing to heavy insurance costs but was revived in 2013 with the help of Blanchardstown Area Partnership and the residents of Strawberry Beds and other local organisations and it was a great success.

Mrs Carroll lived at the bottom of Somerton Lane near Strawberry Hall in 1885. She wrote a poem about the area, mentioning people and places. It's like a mini local history in rhyme. Mrs Carroll mentions Mrs Williams, who was the proprietor of Strawberry Hall, including her own husband, who was an iron moulder by trade. Here is Mrs Carroll's poem:

Mount Sackville Convent is at the head, where young ladies, they are bred,
And taught by nuns of every form, the duties women's life adorn.
Beside it Mr Guinness built a tower. It has a clock strikes every hour.
It can be heard from far and near and gives the working people cheer;
It lets them know the time to quit; they may go home and eat their bit.

Near to that is the Seat of Knowledge, at Castleknock's St Vincent's College,
Where the clergy train up youth, and teach them the love of truth,
And every virtue they require, for the Lord detests a liar,
Even when the truth they tell you can't believe them very well.

All along sweet Anna River, where the playful fishes quiver,
And the anglers patient, stand to try and hook them to the land,
Mrs Williams keeps Strawberry Hall. Never pass without a call.
She is a cheerful kindly woman, and will be glad to see you coming.
Her place was lately renovated, and you will be highly accommodated.

Next at the woolly corner you may stand and take a view around the land,
Carroll's cottage it is there, with flowers around to make it fair.
He is a moulder by his trade, and can show you castings he has made,
It's at the end of Somerton Road that leads to Lady Brooke's abode.
You will see her gates of wide expansion leading to her most lovely mansion

Where a family of the rarest of noble son and daughters fairest –
A loving mother they surround, the greatest blessing to be found
And now lovely grandchildren quite a score, if I could name them many more.
And from the terrace wall can view, all that pass the valley through.

Gibney owns the Anglers' Rest, next Mr Gibney at the hill,
You will never see him standing still; he is always making some improvement.
He gives employment to the poor he never sends them from his door.
Mr Ennis keeps the Wren's Nest, a little further than the rest
And has charming shady bowers, where you might spend some happy hours.

There's also some lovely hills, but sad to see are idle mills
Falling down behind the waters, and our willing sons and daughters,
To another country sped, for to try and earn their bread.

The Wren's Nest today, photograph by author. The Wren's Nest is still going strong and there is traditional music at the weekend and impromptu sessions, barber-shop quartets and pub quizzes.

The River Liffey at Strawberry Beds, c. 1900. The River Liffey rises on Kippure Mountain, just inside the County Wicklow boundary, at a height of 1,800ft. It takes a circuitous route of about 80 miles before entering the sea at Dublin Bay.

Strawberry beds sloping down to the Liffey. Strawberries have been cultivated along this beautiful valley of the River Liffey for over 200 years. In the middle distance is Farmleigh Bridge, also known as Lord Iveagh's Bridge, and Strawberry Beds Bridge. It was built in 1881 to convey water by pipe from the Liffey for Lord Iveagh's livestock. Another pipe conveyed drinking water from a spring well on the south bank for the family at Farmleigh House. Both pipes used a pumping station on the bank of the river to drive the water uphill to the water tower at Farmleigh that doubled as a clock tower. This once beautiful white lattice or truss work steel bridge, designed by the Dublin engineer Wesley William Wilson, has been badly neglected.

The pumping station derived its power from a turbine at the millrace at the Wren's Nest and this source of hydroelectric power also generated electricity for Farmleigh House. The weir also provided power for Coates Ink factory.

In times gone by a linen mill was established at this weir called New Holland Mills. It was built by Dutch settlers. It later became an iron factory.

'Wisteria Cottage,' Strawberry Beds, courtesy Marie Therese Eustace Devitt, photograph by author. If you want to plant a wisteria and enjoy its flowers, do it when you are young as they take their time to flower. This beautiful cottage, with its gorgeous garden and its wonderful wisteria, is about 180 years old, maybe older. I believe it to be the prettiest cottage in Strawberry Beds and there are many pretty cottages in that lovely locality along the bank of the River Liffey.

'Enjoying Strawberries & Cream on the Banks of the Liffey', painting by F. Feld, courtesy Declan Cummins. The painting is based on a photograph taken in the late 1890s, part of the Lawrence Collection. There is some artistic licence as the Liffey flowing through Strawberry Beds is never that close to a road flanked by a cottage.

The cottage itself is near to the Anglers' Rest and is of historical interest. Delia Murphy, the world-renowned singer of Irish songs, lived here. Liam Redmond, the well-known actor who featured in motion pictures such as *Captain Boycott* and *Barry Lyndon* and TV series like *The Avengers*, *Z Cars* and *The Saint*, also lived there with his wife Barbara McDonagh, daughter of 1916 leader Thomas McDonagh.

Mrs Plunkett's Ferry, c. 1930, photograph courtesy Mary Eustace. Mrs Plunkett lived on the Castleknock side of the Liffey opposite Hermitage Golf Club. Her boat service enabled people to take the shortcut across the Liffey and walk up to the Lucan Road to catch the tram into Dublin. It also was used by golfers who lived on the Castleknock side of the Liffey.

A lovely quiet summer's day in Strawberry Beds, c. 1900. You can almost hear the hum of the bees and the chirp of the birds and the waft of the Guinness from Strawberry Hall floating on the gentle wind.

ACKNOWLEDGEMENTS

Many people assisted me in bringing this work to fruition. Some pointed me in the right direction giving advice and information and gave me prints, photographs and paintings. Some captured photographic images and executed paintings and drawings for the book. Others kindly gave me permission to reproduce images in their possession or gave support and encouragement. They all helped make this book possible.

I want to thank the following: Fr Eugene Kennedy who painted some of the beautiful pictures in this book and generously provided a number of the photographs; Gerry Tynan whose knowledge of printing, photography and his expertise in the arcane world of computer technology was invaluable; the late Fr Doyle C.M. of St Vincent's College Castleknock who presented me with a copy of the Centenary Record Book of St. Vincent's College nearly twenty years ago; Cecil Coyne, author of *Dublin 15 and Beyond*, for sharing his knowledge of the Holmpatricks and Abbotstown; David Conway and Bernie O'Shea of the National Sports Campus of Abbotstown who provided much information and granted me access to the campus; Helen Giblin and Deborah Burke of A.D. Wychart & Partners Architects who kindly allowed me to reproduce a panoramic aerial view of Connolly Hospital; Ray Bateson, author of *Memorials of the Easter Rising*, who gave me permission to reproduce his photograph of the James Connolly Memorial; Andrew Lacey who provided photographs of various locations and helped in the enhancement of old photographs that had suffered from age and neglect; RTÉ Stills Library which gave me permission to reproduce two pictures of the Phoenix Park races; 'Blanchardstown Past and Present' and 'Blanchardstown and Surrounding Areas', both local Online Groups, who have gathered a large collection of old pictures in a couple of years;

Olivia Leonard, an administrator with both groups, generously shared a number of images with me relating to Ashtown, Blanchardstown and Cabra; Elizabeth Reid and the extended Reid family for their great pictures relating to Blackhorse Lane/Avenue, Cabra and Ashtown; Robbie Kelly of John G. Rathborne who generously provided me with photographs taken in Rathbornes Candle Factory in 1896; Patrick Walton, formerly of Walton's famous music shop, who spoke to me about his father Martin, a 1916 veteran who founded the company, and generously gave me permission to use photographs; James Langton of Irish Volunteers.org who granted permission for me to use a photograph of Martin Savage; the staff of the National Library of Ireland, National Gallery of Ireland, Gilbert Library, Blanchardstown Library and Fingal Local Studies and Archives in Swords who as usual provided a friendly and efficient service; Ritchie Farrell from Fingle Archives, who gave me so much help back in 1998; Gerry Clabby Heritage Office Fingal County Council for his support and encouragement; Darach Corcoran who carried out a detailed genealogical research into his family and in the process unearthed an amount of historical information on the area which he generously shared with me; Sheila Browne from Castleknock who kindly presented me with two photographs taken in the early 1940s; Phil Parker for his painting of The Hole in the Wall, c. 1995; P.J. McCaffrey of The Hole in the Wall who gave me lots of information about his famous establishment; John Harford of Blanchardstown Brass Band who allowed me to reproduce old photographs of the Band and told me so much of its wonderful history; Joe and Kathleen McGregor who were a great help along with Marie Mulholland; my good friend Liam Delaney who, along with Patsy Kelly, Herbie Hughes, Jim Fay, Tommy Phelan and Paddy Downey, corrected mislabled photographs; Adam Lacey for his drawing of Cardiff's Bridge in 2006 based on an original drawing by B. King in 1837. Martin Coffey, author of *Tell me a Story Cabra Remembered*, who gave me permission to reproduce a picture from his book; Oliver Burns of St Dominic's College who rendered great assistance to me when I was researching the history of the college; Sr Maris Stella O.P., archivist, who also helped with my enquiries; The Honourable Society of King's Inns which gave me permission to reproduce a painting attributed to John Russell of John Toler 1st Earl of Norbury; Tony Jordan of Castleknock Celtic FC who gave me photographs and an account of the history of Castleknock Celtic; Alan Halford who gave me permission to reproduce his infra-red image of The Keep of Tyrell's Castle at Castleknock; Patrick Troy, author of *The Strawberry Beds*, who generously gave me permission to reproduce an image of Somerton House in the early 1900s; Paddy Smith of Luttrellstown Castle for all his assistance in my research of Luttrellstown; Blanchardstown Castleknock History Society including Norah Comiskey and Marie Cummins, who both provided me with old photographs and helped in identifying the people in them, Mary Eustace who gave me photographs of Strawberry Beds and the River Liffey, Mary's daughter Marie Therese Eustace Devitt for allowing me use a photograph of her most delightful residence, Frank O'Connor, chairperson, was a mine of information on the bloodstock industry in the area and also obliged me with a fine drawing of T.K. Laidlaw, Celia Burke who provided me with a beautiful postcard picture of the Vice Regal Lodge 1908 and also helped in my research of Castleknock and Angela Mc Morrow, secretary, who also gave me valuable assistance; *Vanity Fair* magazine for giving me permission to reproduce the image of Major Luke Henry White of Woodlands; the staff and management of Ashtown Castle, Farmleigh House, Ordnance Survey and Aras an Uachtarain; John McCullen, Superintendent Phoenix Park, Margaret McGuirk, Terry Butler, Roy Barron, Joyce Dillon and Maeve Rice for all their help; my old friend the late Brendan Campion for several photographs included in this book; Mary McMenamin who did a lovely painting of the Phoenix Park School for me in 1988; Declan Cummins of Strawberry Hall who generously allowed me to reproduce some of his photographs and paintings; Katie Bracken, sister of Tommy Bracken, who gave me some of her brothers' poems along with photographs of Tommy and Lord Moyne; Tom Mongey who gave me photographs relating to Castleknock Post Office and told me about its history; Donal MacPolin for assisting me in reproducing his beautiful painting of Coolmine House which he presented to Scoil Oilibheir in 2012 and Grainne Ui Chaomhanaigh, school principal, for granting me permission to reproduce Donal's painting; locals Patty Madden, Elizabeth Farnan, Mick Harford, David Manley, and Jack Lovely and Joe McGregor who all helped me in my early research have sadly since passed on to their eternal reward; Beth Amphlett and Ronan Colgan of The History Press Ireland for all their support, advice, and kindness during the preparation of this work.

Finally I want to thank my wife Geraldine who sorted out my grammar, my spelling, my pictures and generally but not always put up with me. Geraldine has put as much into the book as I did so in essence she is the co-author.

BIBLIOGRAPHY

BOOKS AND ARTICLES

Arnold, L.J., *The Restoration Land Settlement in Co. Dublin* (Irish Academic Press, 1993)

Anonymous, *Annals of the Dominican Convent of St. Mary's Cabra with some Account of its Origin 1647-1912* (St Mary's Dominican Convent Cabra, 1913)

Ball, F.E., *History of County Dublin* (Gill & Macmillan, 1906)

Barton, Brian, *The Secret Court Martial Records of the Easter Rising* (The History Press, 2010)

Bateson, Ray, *Memorials of the Easter Rising* (Irish Graves Publications 2013)

Behan, Anthony P., *Our Lady Help of Christians Celebrating 50 Years 1952-2002* (Golden Jubilee Committee of Our Lady Help of Christians Parish, 2002)

Bennett, Richard, *The Black and Tans* (Barnes & Noble, 1995)

Breen, Dan, *My Fight for Irish Freedom* (Mercier Press, 1981)

Brook, Raymond F., *The Brimming River* (Allen Figgis, 1961)

Burns, Oliver & Wilson, Mairin, *Dominican Sisters Cabra 1819-1994* (Dominican Sisters, Cabra, 1994)

Byrne, Joseph, *Byrnes Dictionary of Irish Local History* (Mercier Press, 2004)

Cafferky, John & Hannafin, Kevin, *Scandal & Betrayal, Shackleton & The Irish Crown Jewels* (The Collins Press, 2002)

Campbell, C.M., *Fr. John Editor of St. Vincent's College Castleknock Centenary Records 1835-1935* (St Vincent's College, 1935)

Clarke, Peter, *The Royal Canal: The Complete Story* (Elo Publications, 1992)

Coffey, Martin, *Tell Me a Story Cabra Remembered* (Choice Publishing, 2013)

Collins, M.E., *Conquest & Colonisation* (Gill & Macmillan, 1969)

Connell, Joseph E.A., *Dublin in Rebellion A Directory 1913-1923* (Lilliput Press 2006)

Coots, R.J., *The Middle Ages* (Longman Group, 1972)

Corfe, Tom, *The Phoenix Park Murders* (Hodder & Stoughton, 1968)

Cosgrave, Dillon, *North Dublin City & Environs* (Gill, 1909)

Coyne, Cecil, *Dublin 15 and Beyond* (Blanchardstown Tidy Towns Committee, 2003)

Cronin, Elizabeth, *Convent of the Incarnation Blanchardstown 1828-1858*
    (Self-published, 2008)

Cronin, Elizabeth, *Charting Change Blanchardstown 1837-2012* (Self-published 2012)

Cullen, C., and Kelly, P.A., *A History of St. Brigid's Church, Blanchardstown
    1837-1987* (Blanchardstown Printing and Publishing, 1997)

Curran, Simon, *A Short History of Dunsinea House* (An Foras Taluntais, 1984)

D'Alton, John, *History of County Dublin* (Tower Books, 1976)

Delaney, Mary, *Mount Sackville 1864-2004* (Sisters of St Joseph of Cluny, 2004)

Delaney, Ruth and Bath, Ian, *Ireland's Royal Canal 1789-2009* (Lilliput Press, 2010)

Fanning, Ronan, *Fatal Path British Government and Irish Revolution 1910-1922*
    (Faber and Faber, 2013)

Farnan, J., 'Notes on War of Independence & Civil War', unpublished notes held
    privately by Marie Cummins, relative of J. Farnan.

Ferriter, Diarmaid, *The Transformation of Ireland 1900-2000* (Profile Books, 2005)

Fingall, Elizabeth Countess of and Pamela Hinkson, *Seventy Years Young Memories
    of Elizabeth Countess of Fingal* (Lilliput Press, 1991)

Finglas Through the Ages (Finglas Environmental Heritage Project, 1991)

Gardiner, Juliet, *Who's Who in British History* (Ciro Books, 2002)

Gray, Tony, *The Lost Years The Emergency in Ireland 1939-45* (Warner Books, 1998)

Herlihy, Jim, *The Royal Irish Constabulary* (Four Courts Press, 1999)

Hickey, D.J., & Doherty, J.E., *A New Dictionary of Irish History from 1800* (Gill &
    MacMillan, 2005)

Jordan, Anthony J., *Churchill A Founder of Modern Ireland* (Westport Books, 1995)

Joyce, P. Weston, *Irish Local Names Explained* (Fitzhouse Books, 1990)

Joyce, Weston St John, *The Neighbourhood of Dublin* (Hughes & Hughes, 1912)

Judge, Jacinta, *Fingal Through Old Picture Postcards* (Fingal County Libraries 2009)

Keegan, John and Wheatcroft, Andrew, *Who's Who in Military History*
    (Hutchinson, 1987)

Kirkpatrick, Alexander De Lapere, *Chronicles of the Kirkpatrick Family* (T. Moring of
    the De La More Press, London)

Lacey, Jim, *A Candle in the Window* (Mercier Press, 2007)

Lenihan, Padraig, *The Battle of the Boyne, 1690* (Tempus Publishing Ltd, 2005)

Lewis, Samuel, *Lewis's Topographical Dictionary* (1837)

Liddy, Pat, *History of Ongar* (Self-published, 2001)

Lyons, Mary, *The Memoirs of Mrs Leeson Madam* (Lilliput Press 1995)

Mackey, Rex, *Windward of the Law* (Roundhall Press, 1992)

MacCurtain, Brian and Tiernan, Mary *Adsilita* (Chapelizod Heritage Society
Historical Journal, 2010)

McC. Dix., E.R., 'The Lesser Castles of Dublin', *Irish Builder
Magazine* (1898)

McCullen, Dr. John A., *An Illustrated History of the Phoenix Park Landscape and
    Management to 1880* (Government Publications Office of Public Works, 2009)

McLoughlin, E.P., *Castleknock Skeletal Material* (Stationery Office Dublin, 1950)

McMahon, Finn, 'When Handball Made Headlines', series of articles in *Licensed
    Vintners Magazine* (1968)

McNally, Vincent J., *Reform, Revolution & Reaction* (University Press of America, 1930)

McNally, Michael, *The Battle of Aughrim 1691* (The History Press, 2008)

MacPolin, Donal, Sobolewski, Peter, *Blanchardstown, Castleknock and the Park, Paintings & Stories 'twixt Liffey & Tolka* (Cottage Publications, 2001)

Meagher, Revd John and M.G., *Historical Notes Caeveen and Early Parish* (Graham Cumming, The Church Publishers, 1954)

Milne, Kenneth, *Short History of the Church of Ireland* (Columba Press, 2003)

Moloney, Senan, *The Phoenix Park Murders* (Mercier Press, 2006)

Mulvihill, Mary, *Ingenious Ireland* (Town House & Country House Ltd, 2002)

Musgrave, Bart., *Sir Richard, Musgrave's Irish Rebellion* ed. J. Milliken (Self published, 1799)

Neary, Bernard, *A History of Cabra and Phibsboro* (Lenhar Community Press, 1984)

Neary, Bernard, *Dublin 7* (Lenhar Publications, 1992)

Neary, Bernard, *The Candle Factory* (The Lilliput Press, 1998)

Neeson, Eoin, *The Civil War 1922-23* (Poolbeg, 1989)

Nevin, Donal, *James Connolly 'A Full Life'* (Gill & Macmillan, 2006)

Nolan, Brendan, *Phoenix Park A History and Guidebook* (The Liffey Press, 2006)

O'Beirne, J.W., *History of Phoenix Park* (Pearl Printing Company, 1911, reprinted 1930)

O'Broin, Leon, *W.E. Wylie and the Irish Revolution 1916-1921* (Gill & Macmillan, 1989)

O'Connor, Nessa, *Palmerstown An Ancient Place* (Environment Publications, 2003)

O'Driscoll, James, *Cnucha: A History of Castleknock* (Self published, 1977)

O'Reardon, Revd W., *Historical Notes of St. Brigid's Yearbook*

Priestly, Ciaran, *Clonsilla & The Rebellion of 1798* (Maynooth Studies in Local History Four Courts Press, 2009)

Quigley, Patrick, *The Polish Irishman The Life and Times of Casimir Markievicz* (Liffey Press, 2012)

Reportorium Novum, *Dublin Diocesan Historical Record* (Veritas, 1971)

Roche, Richard, *The Norman Invasion of Ireland* (Anvil Books, 1995)

The Royal Canal, OPW

Troy, Patrick, *The Strawberry Beds* (Original Writing, 2013)

Rutty, John, *Natural History of Co. Dublin* (Self published, 1772)

Sebba, Anne, *Jenny Churchill Winston's American Mother* (John Murray Publisher, 2007)

Simms, J.G., *The Jacobite Parliament of 1689* (Dundalgan Press, 1966)

Sobolewski, Peter & Langran, Colin, *Blanchardstown Chronicle* (Coolmine Community College, 1992)

Somerville, Large, Peter, *Dublin the Fair City* (Sinclair Stevenson, 1996)

Sweeney, Clair J., *The Rivers of Dublin* (Dublin Corporation, 1992)

Townshend, Charles, *Easter 1916 The Irish Rebellion* (Penguin Books, 2006)

Various, *Dictionary of National Biography* (Oxford University Press, 1937)

Various, *Viking Settlements in Medieval Dublin* (Department of Environmental Studies, UCD, 1978)

Wall, Maureen, *The Penal Laws 1691-1700* (Dundalgan Press, 1976)
Wayman, Patrick A., *Dunsink Observatory* (Dublin Institute for Advanced Studies, 1979)
Wilson, A.N., *The Victorians* (Arrow Books, 2002)
Wren, Jimmy, *The Villages of Dublin* (Tomar Publishing, 1988)

NEWSPAPERS AND PERIODICALS

Dublin Historical Records
Dublin Penny Journal 1832-1836
Evening Mail
Evening Telegraph
Freeman's Journal
Illustrated London News
Newswest Yearbook (1995-96), Kelly Freida, editor
The Irish Times
The Tolka (Dublin University magazine)

PAPERS READ TO ROYAL SOCIETY OF ANTIQUARIES OF IRELAND

'The Grant of Castleknock to Hugh Tyrell,' Brooks, Eric St John, 1933
'The Tyrells of Castleknock,' Brooks, Eric St John, 1946

PAPERS READ TO OLD DUBLIN SOCIETY

'An Outline for the Life of Warren of Corduff,' Little, George A., 1968
'Norbury, "The Hanging Judge,"' Lysaight, Moira, 1975
'Dr Carpenter,' MacGiolla Padraig, Brian, 1976
'John Troy,' Purcell, Mary 1976
'J. Sheridan Le Fanu's Chapelizod & Dublin Connection, Brennan, Kevin, 1979

RECOMMENDED ONLINE WEBSITES AND OTHER REPOSITORIES OF RECORDS

Baptismal, Marriage and Burial Records of St Brigid's Parish, Blanchardstown, 1774-1780
Baptismal and Marriage Records of Nativity of Blessed Virgin Mary Parish, Chapelizod, 1849-1901
Blanchardstown Library (in particular the Reference Section)
Brookeborough Papers (Public Records Office Northern Ireland) available online from www.proni.gov.uk
Burke's Peerage www.burkespeerage.com
Census Returns 1901 and 1911
Dublin City Council Library, Navan Road, Cabra, Dublin 7
Fingal Local Studies Library and Archives Swords
Fr Michael Dungan's Diary of Parish Priest of Blanchardstown 1836-1868 held in the parish archives

Gilbert Library with Dublin City Public Libraries and Archives, Pearse Street, Dublin 2

Griffith's Valuation County of Dublin July 1851

Irish Voluteers.org

National Archives of Ireland, Bishop Street Dublin 8 (www.nationalarchives.ie)

National Gallery of Ireland, Merrion Square Dublin 2 (www.nationalgallery.ie)

National Library of Ireland, Kildare Street Dublin 2 (www.nli.ie)

Ordnance Survey Letters by John Donovan. Donated by Ordnance Survey 1861 to Royal Irish Academy Library. Digital versions are accessible at www.askaboutireland.ie

Porter's Guide and Directory North County Dublin 1912

The Down Survey, 1655, work carried out by Sir William Petty for Surveyor General's Office in Dublin, completed 1658. Trinity College Dublin has an on line version of The Down Survey at http://downsurveytcd.ie/indexhtml

The Irish Folklore Commission, UCD, Belfield

The Past and Present Blanchardstown and Surrounding Areas – Online History Group

Tithe Applotment Books

Thom's Directories (various)

www.blanchardstownbrassband.com

www.farmleigh.ie

www.phoenixpark.ie

INDEX